Monologues from Shakespeare's First Folio for Women: *The Comedies*

The Applause Shakespeare Monologue Series

T0346655

Other Shakespeare Titles From Applause

Once More unto the Speech Dear Friends
Volume One: The Comedies
Compiled and Edited with Commentary by Neil Freeman

Once More unto the Speech Dear Friends
Volume Two: The Histories
Compiled and Edited with Commentary by Neil Freeman

Once More unto the Speech Dear Friends
Volume Three: The Tragedies
Compiled and Edited with Commentary by Neil Freeman

The Applause First Folio in Modern Type
Prepared and Annotated by Neil Freeman

The Folio Texts
Prepared and Annotated by Neil Freeman, Each of the 36 plays of the
Applause First Folio in Modern Type individually bound

The Applause Shakespeare Library
Plays of Shakespeare Edited for Performance

Soliloquy: The Shakespeare Monologues

Monologues from Shakespeare's First Folio for Women:
The Comedies

Compilation and Commentary by
Neil Freeman

Edited by
Paul Sugarman

APPLAUSE
THEATRE & CINEMA BOOKS

Guilford, Connecticut

APPLAUSE
THEATRE & CINEMA BOOKS

An imprint of Globe Pequot, the trade division of
The Rowman & Littlefield Publishing Group, Inc.
4501 Forbes Blvd., Ste. 200
Lanham, MD 20706
www.rowman.com

Distributed by NATIONAL BOOK NETWORK

Library of Congress Cataloging-in-Publication Data available

Library of Congress Control Number: 2021944380

ISBN 978-1-4930-5682-8 (paperback)
ISBN 978-1-4930-5683-5 (ebook)

♾™ The paper used in this publication meets the minimum requirements of
American National Standard for Information Sciences—Permanence of Paper for
Printed Library Materials, ANSI/NISO Z39.48-1992

Dedication

Although Neil Freeman passed to that "undiscovered country" in 2015, his work continues to lead students and actors to a deeper understanding of Shakespeare's plays. With the exception of Shakespeare's words (and my humble foreword), the entirety of the material within these pages is Neil's. May these editions serve as a lasting legacy to a life of dedicated scholarship, and a great passion for Shakespeare.

Contents

Foreword *11*

Preface and Brief Background. *15*

Introduction *19*

How these texts work *27*

Adrianna, *The Comedie of Errors.* *33*

Curtizan, *The Comedie of Errors* *37*

Julia, *The Two Gentlemen of Verona* *41*

Julia, *The Two Gentlemen of Verona* *45*

Sylvia, *The Two Gentlemen of Verona* *49*

Julia, *The Two Gentlemen of Verona* *53*

Princess, *Loves Labour's Lost.* *57*

Rosaline, *Loves Labour's Lost* *61*

Princess, *Loves Labour's Lost.* *65*

Hermia, *A Midsommer Nights Dreame* *69*

Helena, *A Midsommer Nights Dreame.* *73*

Queene, *A Midsommer Nights Dreame* *77*

Helena, *A Midsommer Nights Dreame*. *81*

Hermia, *A Midsommer Nights Dreame* *85*

Titania, *A Midsommer Nights Dreame* *89*

Helena, *A Midsommer Nights Dreame*. *93*

Jessica, *The Merchant of Venice*. *97*

Portia, *The Merchant of Venice*. *101*

Portia, *The Merchant of Venice*. *105*

Beatrice, *Much Adoe About Nothing* *109*

Hero, *Much Adoe About Nothing*. *113*

Mistress Page, *The Merry Wives of Windsor* *117*

Celia, *As You Like It* *121*

Rosalind, *As You Like It*. *125*

Phebe, *As You Like It* *129*

Rosalind, *As You Like It*. *133*

Viola,*Twelfe Night, or, what you will*. *137*

Olivia,*Twelfe Night, or, what you will*. *141*

Viola, *Twelfe Night, or, what you will*. *145*

Olivia, *Twelfe Night, or, what you will* *149*

Hellen, *Alls Well That Ends Well* *153*

Hellen, *Alls Well That Ends Well* *157*

Diana, *Alls Well That Ends Well*.........................*161*

Hermione, *The Winter's Tale*............................*165*

Hermione, *The Winter's Tale*............................*169*

Miranda, *The Tempest*..................................*173*

Bibliography...*179*

Appendix 1: Guide to the Early Texts *183*

Appendix 2: Words, Words, Words........................*184*

Appendix 3: The Pattern of Magic *187*

Acknowledgments.......................................*189*

Author Bio *190*

FOREWORD

Paul Sugarman

Monologues from Shakespeare's First Folio presents the work of Neil Freeman, longtime champion of Shakespeare's First Folio, whose groundbreaking explorations into how first printings offered insights to the text in rehearsals, stage and in the classroom. This work continued with *Once More Unto the Speech Dear Friends: Monologues from Shakespeare's First Folio with Modern Text Versions for Comparison* where Neil collected over 900 monologues divided between the Comedy, History and Tragedy Published by Applause in three masterful volumes which present the original First Folio text side by side with the modern, edited version of the text. These volumes provide a massive amount of material and information. However both the literary scope, and the literal size of these volumes can be intimidating and overwhelming. This series' intent is to make the work more accessible by taking material from the encyclopediac original volumes and presenting it in an accessible workbook format.

To better focus the work for actors and students the texts are contrasted side by side with introductory notes before and commentary after to aid the exploration of the text. By comparing modern and First Folio printings, Neil points the way to gain new insights into Shakespeare's text. Editors over the centuries have "corrected" and updated the texts to make them "accessible," or "grammatically correct." In doing so they have lost vital clues and information that Shakespeare placed there for his actors. With the texts side by side, you can see where and why editors have made changes and what may have been lost in translation.

In addition to being divided into Histories, Comedies, and Tragedies, the original series further breaks down speeches by the character's designated gender, also indicating speeches appropriate for any gender. Drawing from this example, this series breaks down each original volume into four workbooks: speeches for Women of all ages, Younger Men, Older Men and Any Gender. Gender is naturally fluid for Shakespeare's characters since during his time, ALL of the characters were portrayed by males. Contemporary productions of Shakespeare commonly switch character genders (Prospero has become Prospera), in addition to presenting single gender, reverse gender and gender non-specific productions. There are certainly characters and speeches where the gender is immaterial, hence the inclusion of a volume of speeches for Any Gender. This was something that Neil had indicated in the original volumes; we are merely following his example.

Once More Unto the Speech Dear Friends was a culmination of Neil's dedicated efforts to make the First Folio more accessible and available to readers and to illuminate for actors the many clues within the Folio text, as originally published. The material in this book is drawn from that work and retains Neil's British spelling of words (i.e. capitalisation) and his extensive commentary on each speech. Neil went on to continue this work as a master teacher of Shakespeare with another series of Shakespeare editions, his 'rhythm texts' and the ebook that he published on Apple Books, *The Shakespeare Variations.*

Neil published on his own First Folio editions of the plays in modern type which were the basis the Folio Texts series published by Applause of all 36 plays in the First Folio. These individual editions all have extensive notes on the changes that modern editions had made. This material was then combined to create a complete reproduction of the First Folio in modern type, *The Applause First Folio of Shakespeare in Modern Type.* These editions make the First Folio more accessible than ever before. The examples in this book demonstrate how the clues from the First Folio will give insights to understanding and performing these speeches and why it is a worthwhile endeavour to discover the riches in the First Folio.

PREFACE AND BRIEF BACKGROUND TO THE FIRST FOLIO

WHY ANOTHER SERIES OF SOLILOQUY BOOKS?

There has been an enormous change in theatre organisation recent in the last twenty years. While the major large-scale companies have continued to flourish, many small theatre companies have come into being, leading to

- much doubling
- cross gender casting, with many one time male roles now being played legitimately by/as women in updated time-period productions
- young actors being asked to play leading roles at far earlier points in their careers

All this has meant actors should be able to demonstrate enormous flexibility rather than one limited range/style. In turn, this has meant

- a change in audition expectations
- actors are often expected to show more range than ever before
- often several shorter audition speeches are asked for instead of one or two longer ones
- sometimes the initial auditions are conducted in a shorter amount of time

Thus, to stay at the top of the game, the actor needs more knowledge of what makes the play tick, especially since

- early plays demand a different style from the later ones
- the four genres (comedy, history, tragedy, and the peculiar romances) all have different acting/textual requirements
- parts originally written for the older, more experienced actors again require a different approach from those written for the younger

ones, as the young roles, especially the female ones, were played by young actors extraordinarily skilled in the arts of rhetoric

There's now much more knowledge of how the original quarto and folio texts can add to the rehearsal exploration/acting and directing process as well as to the final performance.

Each speech is made up of four parts

- a background to the speech, placing it in the context of the play, and offering line length and an approximate timing to help you choose what might be right for any auditioning occasion
- a modern text version of the speech, with the sentence structure clearly delineated side by side with
- a folio version of the speech, where modern texts changes to the capitalization, spelling and sentence structure can be plainly seen
- a commentary explaining the differences between the two texts, and in what way the original setting can offer you more information to explore

Thus if they wish, **beginners** can explore just the background and the modern text version of the speech.

An actor experienced in exploring the Folio can make use of the background and the Folio version of the speech

And those wanting to know as many details as possible and how they could help define the deft stepping stones of the arc of the speech can use all four elements on the page.

The First Folio

(FOR LIST OF CURRENT REPRODUCTIONS SEE BIBLIOGRAPHY

The end of 1623 saw the publication of the justifiably famed First Folio (F1). The single volume, published in a run of approximately 1,000 copies at the princely sum of one pound (a tremendous risk, considering that a single play would sell at no more than six pence, one fortieth of F1's price, and that the annual salary of a schoolmaster was only ten pounds), contained thirty-six plays.

The manuscripts from which each F1 play would be printed came from a variety of sources. Some had already been printed. Some came from the playhouse complete with production details. Some had no theatrical input at all, but were handsomely copied out and easy to read. Some were supposedly very messy, complete with first draft scribbles and crossings out. Yet, as Charlton Hinman, the revered dean of First Folio studies describes F1 in the Introduction to the Norton Facsimile:

> It is of inestimable value for what it is, for what it contains. For here are preserved the masterworks of the man universally recognized as our greatest writer; and preserved, as Ben Jonson realized at the time of the original publication, not for an age but for all time.

WHAT DOES F1 REPRESENT?

- texts prepared for actors who rehearsed three days for a new play and one day for one already in the repertoire
- written in a style (rhetoric incorporating debate) so different from ours (grammatical) that many modern alterations based on grammar (or poetry) have done remarkable harm to the rhetorical/debate quality of the original text and thus to interpretations of characters at key moments of stress.
- written for an acting company the core of which steadily grew older, and whose skills and interests changed markedly over twenty years as well as for an audience whose make-up and interests likewise changed as the company grew more experienced

The whole is based upon supposedly the best documents available at the time, collected by men closest to Shakespeare throughout his career, and brought to a single printing house whose errors are now widely understood - far more than those of some of the printing houses that produced the original quartos.

TEXTUAL SOURCES FOR THE AUDITION SPEECHES
Individual modern editions consulted in the preparation of the Modern Text version of the speeches are listed in the Bibliography under the separate headings 'The Complete Works in Compendium Format' and ' The Complete Works in Separate Individual Volumes.' Most of the modern versions of the speeches are a compilation of several of these texts. However, all modern act, scene and/or line numbers refer the reader to The Riverside Shakespeare, in my opinion still the best of the complete works despite the excellent compendiums that have been published since.

The First Folio versions of the speeches are taken from a variety of already published sources, including not only all the texts listed in the 'Photostatted Reproductions in Compendium Format' section of the Bibliography, but also earlier, individually printed volumes, such as the twentieth century editions published under the collective title *The Facsimiles of Plays from The First Folio of Shakespeare* by Faber & Gwyer, and the nineteenth century editions published on behalf of The New Shakespeare Society.

INTRODUCTION

So, congratulations , you've got an audition, and for a Shakespeare play no less.

You've done all your homework, including, hopefully , reading the whole play to see the full range and development of the character.

You've got an idea of the character, the situation in which you/it finds itself (the given circumstance s); what your/its needs are (objectives/ intentions); and what you intend to do about them (action /tactics).

You've looked up all the unusual words in a good dictionary or glossary; you've turned to a well edited modern edition to find out what some of the more obscure references mean.

And those of you who understand metre and rhythm have worked on the poetic values of the speech, and you are word perfect . . .

. . . and yet it's still not working properly and/or you feel there's more to be gleaned from the text , but you're not sure what that something is or how to go about getting at it; in other words, all is not quite right, yet.

THE KEY QUESTION

What text have you been working with - a good modern text or an 'original' text, that is a copy of one of the first printings of the play?

If it's a modern text, no matter how well edited (and there are some splendid single copy editions available, see the Bibliography for further details), despite all the learned information offered, it's not surprising you feel somewhat at a loss, for there is a huge difference between the original printings (the First Folio, and the individual quartos, see

Appendix 1 for further details) and any text prepared after 1700 right up to the most modern of editions. All the post 1700 texts have been tidied-up for the modern reader to ingest silently, revamped according to the rules of correct grammar, syntax and poetry. However the 'originals' were prepared for actors speaking aloud playing characters often in a great deal of emotional and/or intellectual stress, and were set down on paper according to the very flexible rules of rhetoric and a seemingly very cavalier attitude towards the rules of grammar, and syntax, and spelling, and capitalisation, and even poetry.

Unfortunately, because of the grammatical and syntactical standardisation in place by the early 1700's, many of the quirks and oddities of the origin also have been dismissed as 'accidental' - usually as compositor error either in deciphering the original manuscript, falling prey to their own particular idosyncracies, or not having calculated correctly the amount of space needed to set the text. Modern texts dismiss the possibility that these very quirks and oddities may be by Shakespeare, hearing his characters in as much difficulty as poor Peter Quince is in *A Midsummer Night's Dream* (when he, as the Prologue, terrified and struck down by stage fright, makes a huge grammatical hash in introducing his play 'Pyramus and Thisbe' before the aristocracy, whose acceptance or otherwise, can make or break him)

> If we offend, it is with our good will.
> That you should think, we come not to offend,
> But with good will.
> > To show our simple skill,
> That is the true beginning of our end .
> Consider then, we come but in despite.
> We do not come, as minding to content you ,
> Our true intent is.
> > All for your delight
> We are not here.
> > That you should here repent you,

The Actors are at hand; and by their show,
You shall know all, that you are like to know.

(A Midsummer Night's Dream)

In many other cases in the complete works what was originally printed is equally 'peculiar,' but, unlike Peter Quince , these peculiarities are usually regularised by most modern texts.

However, this series of volumes is based on the belief - as the following will show - that most of these 'peculiarities' resulted from Shakespeare setting down for his actors the stresses, trials, and tribulations the characters are experiencing as they think and speak, and thus are theatrical gold-dust for the actor, director, scholar, teacher, and general reader alike.

THE FIRST ESSENTIAL DIFFERENCE BETWEEN THE TWO TEXTS

THINKING

A **modern** text can show
- the story line
- your character's conflict with the world at large
- your character's conflict with certain individuals within that world

but because of the very way an 'original' text was set, it can show you all this plus one key extra, the very thing that makes big speeches what they are

- the conflict within the character

WHY?

Any good playwright writes about characters in stressful situations who are often in a state of conflict not only with the world around them and the people in that world, but also within themselves. And you probably know from personal experience that when these conflicts occur people do not necessarily utter the most perfect of grammatical/poetic/syntactic statements, phrases, or sentences. Joy and delight, pain and sorrow often come sweeping through in the way things are said, in the incoherence of the phrases, the running together of normally disassociated ideas, and even in the sounds of the words themselves.

The tremendous advantage of the period in which Shakespeare was setting his plays down on paper and how they first appeared in print was that when characters were rational and in control of self and situation, their phrasing and sentences (and poetic structure) would appear to be quite normal even to a modern eye - but when things were going wrong, so sentences and phrasing (and poetic structure) would become highly erratic. But the Quince type eccentricities are rarely allowed to stand. Sadly, in tidying, most modern texts usually make the text far too clean, thus setting rationality when none originally existed.

THE SECOND ESSENTIAL DIFFERENCE BETWEEN THE TWO TEXTS
SPEAKING, ARGUING, DEBATING

Having discovered what and how you/your character is thinking is only the first stage of the work - you/it then have to speak aloud, in a society that absolutely loved to speak - and not only speak ideas (content) but to speak entertainingly so as to keep listeners enthralled (and this was especially so when you have little content to offer and have to mask it somehow - think of today 's television adverts and political spin doctors as a parallel and you get the picture). Indeed one of the Elizabethan 'how to win an argument' books was very precise about this - George Puttenham, *The Art of English Poesie* (1589).

A: ELIZABETHAN SCHOOLING

All educated classes could debate/argue at the drop of a hat, for both boys (in 'petty-schools') and girls (by books and tutors) were trained in what was known overall as the art of rhetoric, which itself was split into three parts

- first, how to distinguish the real from false appearances/outward show (think of the three caskets in *The Merchant of Venice* where the language on the gold and silver caskets enticingly, and deceptively, seems to offer hopes of great personal rewards that are dashed when the language is carefully explored, whereas once the apparent threat on the lead casket is carefully analysed the reward therein is the greatest that could be hoped for)
- second, how to frame your argument on one of 'three great grounds'; honour/morality; justice/legality; and, when all else fails, expedience/practicality.
- third, how to order and phrase your argument so winsomely that your audience will vote for you no matter how good the opposition - and there were well over two hundred rules and variations by which winning could be achieved, all of which had to be assimilated before a child's education was considered over and done with.

B: THINKING ON YOUR FEET: I.E. THE QUICK, DEFT , RAPID MODIFICATION OF EACH TINY THOUGHT

The Elizabethan/therefore your character/therefore you were also trained to explore and modify your thoughts as you spoke - never would you see a sentence in its entirety and have it perfectly worked out in your mind before you spoke (unless it was a deliberately written, formal public declaration, as with the Officer of the Court in The Winter' s Tale, reading the charges against Hermione). Thus after uttering your very first phrase, you might expand it, or modify it, deny it, change it, and so on throughout the whole sentence and speech.

Neil Freeman

From the poet Samuel Coleridge Taylor there is a wonderful description of how Shakespeare puts thoughts together like "a serpent twisting and untwisting in its own strength," that is, with one thought springing out of the one previous. Treat each new phrase as a fresh unravelling of the serpent's coil. What is discovered (and therefore said) is only revealed as the old coil/phrase disappears revealing a new coil in its place. The new coil is the new thought. The old coil moves/disappears because the previous phrase is finished with as soon as it is spoken.

C: MODERN APPLICATION

It is very rarely we speak dispassionately in our 'real' lives, after all thoughts give rise to feelings, feelings give rise to thoughts, and we usually speak both together - unless

1/ we're trying very hard for some reason to control ourselves and not give ourselves away

2/ or the volcano of emotions within us is so strong that we cannot control ourselves, and feelings swamp thoughts

3/ and sometimes whether deliberately or unconsciously we colour words according to our feelings; the humanity behind the words so revealed is instantly understandable.

D: HOW THE ORIGINAL TEXTS NATURALLY ENHANCE/ UNDERSCORE THIS CONTROL OR RELEASE

The amazing thing about the way all Elizabethan/early Jacobean texts were first set down (the term used to describe the printed words on the page being 'orthography'), is that it was flexible, it allowed for such variations to be automatically set down without fear of grammatical repercussion.

So if Shakespeare heard Juliet's nurse working hard to try to convince Juliet that the Prince's nephew Juliet is being forced to (bigamously) marry, instead of setting the everyday normal

'O he's a lovely gentleman'

which the modern texts HAVE to set, the first printings were permitted to set

'O hee's a Lovely Gentleman'

suggesting that something might be going on inside the Nurse that causes her to release such excessive extra energy.

E: BE CAREFUL

This needs to be stressed very carefully: the orthography doesn't dictate to you/force you to accept exactly what it means. The orthography simply suggests you might want to explore this moment further or more deeply.

In other words, simply because of the flexibility with which the Elizabethans/Shakespeare could set down on paper what they heard in their minds or wanted their listeners to hear, in addition to all the modern acting necessities of character - situation, objective, intention, action, and tactics the original Shakespeare texts offer pointers to where feelings (either emotional or intellectual, or when combined together as passion, both) are also evident.

SUMMARY

BASIC APPROACH TO THE SPEECHES SHOWN BELOW

(after reading the 'background')

1/ first use the modem version shown in the first column: by doing so you can discover
- the basic plot line of what's happening to the character, and
- the first set of conflicts/obstacles impinging on the character as a result of the situation or actions of other characters
- the supposed grammatical and poetical correctnesses of the speech

2/ then you can explore
- any acting techniques you'd apply to any modem soliloquy, including establishing for the character
- the given circumstances of the scene
- their outward state of being (who they are sociologically, etc.)
- their intentions and objectives
- the resultant action and tactics they decide to pursue

3/ when this is complete, turn to the First Folio version of the text, shown on the facing page: this will help you discover and explore
- the precise thinking and debating process so essential to an understanding of any Shakespeare text
- the moments when the text is NOT grammatically or poetically as correct as the modern texts would have you believe, which will in tum help you recognise
- the moments of conflict and struggle stemming from within the character itself
- the sense of fun and enjoyment the Shakespeare language nearly always offers you no matter how dire the situation

4/ should you wish to further explore even more the differences between the two texts, the commentary that follows discusses how the First Folio has been changed, and what those alterations might mean for the human arc of the speech

NOTES ON HOW THESE SPEECHES ARE SET UP

For each of the speeches the first page will include the Background on the speech and other information including number of lines, approximate timing and who is addressed. Then will follow a spread which shows the modern text version on the left and the First Folio version on the right, followed by a page of Commentary.

PROBABLE TIMING: (shown on the Background page before the speeches begin, set below the number of lines) 0.45 = a forty-five second speech

SYMBOLS & ABBREVIATIONS IN THE COMMENTARY AND TEXT

F: the First Folio

mt.: modern texts

F # followed by a number: the number of the sentence under discussion in the First Folio version of the speech, thus F #7 would refer to the seventh sentence

mt. # followed by a numb er: the number of the sentence under discussion in the modern text version of the speech, thus mt. #5 would refer to the fifth sentence

 # /#, (e.g. 3/7): the first number refers to the number of capital letters in the passage under discussion; the second refers to the number of long spellings therein

within a quotation from the speech: / indicates where one verse line ends and a fresh one starts

[ ] : set around words in both texts when F1 sets one word , mt another

{ } : some minor alteration has been made, in a speech built up, where, a word or phrase will be changed, added, or removed

{†} : this symbol shows where a sizeable part of the text is omitted

TERMS FOUND IN THE COMMENTARY
OVERALL

1/ **orthography**: the capitalization, spellings, punctuation of the First Folio
SIGNS OF IMPORTANT DISCOVERIES/ARGUMENTS WITHIN A FIRST FOLIO SPEECH

2/ **major punctuation**: colons and semicolons: since the Shakespeare texts are based so much on the art of debate and argument, the importance of F1 's major punctuation must not be underestimated, for both the semi-colon (;) and colon (:) mark a moment of importance for the character, either for itself, as a moment of discovery or revelation, or as a key point in a discussion, argument or debate that it wishes to impress upon other characters onstage

as a rule of thumb:

a/ the more frequent colon (:) suggests that whatever the power of the point discovered or argued, the character is not side-tracked and can continue with the argument - as such, the colon can be regarded as a **logical** connection

b/ the far less frequent semicolon (;) suggests that because of the power inherent in the point discovered or argued, the character is side-tracked and momentarily loses the argument and falls back into itself or can only continue the argument with great difficulty - as such, the semicolon should be regarded as an **emotional** connection

3/ **surround phrases**: phrase(s) surrounded by major punctuation, or a combination of major punctuation and the end or beginning of a sentence: thus these phrases seem to be of especial importance for both character and speech, well worth exploring as key to the argument made and /or emotions released

DIALOGUE NOT FOUND IN THE FIRST FOLIO
∞ set where modern texts add dialogue from a quarto text which has not been included in Fl

A LOOSE RULE OF THUMB TO THE THINKING PROCESS OF A FIRST FOLIO CHARACTER

1/ mental discipline/**intellect**: a section where capitals dominate suggests that the intellectual reason ing behind what is being spoken or discovered is of more concern than the personal response beneath it

2/ feelings/**emotions**: a section where long spellings dominate suggests that the personal response to what is being spoken or discovered is of more concern than the intellectual reasoning behind it

3/ **passion**: a section where both long spellings and capitals are present in almost equal proportions suggests that both mind and emotion/feelings are inseparable, and thus the character is speaking passionately

SIGNS OF LESS THAN GRAMMATICAL THINKING WITHIN A FIRST FOLIO SPEECH

1/ **onrush**: sometimes thoughts are coming so fast that several topics are joined together as one long sentence suggesting that the F character's mind is working very quickly, or that his/her emotional state is causing some concern: most mod ern texts split such a sentence into several grammatically correct parts (the opening speech of *As You Like It* is a fine example, where F's long 18 line opening sentence is split into six): while the modern texts' resetting may be syntactically correct, the F moment is nowhere near as calm as the revisions suggest

2/ **fast-link**: sometimes F shows thoughts moving so quickly for a character that the connecting punctuation between disparate topics is merely a comma, suggesting that there is virtually no pause in springing from one idea to the next: unfortunately most modern texts rarely allow this to stand, instead replacing the obviously disturbed comma with a grammatical period, once more creating calm that it seems the original texts never intended to show

FIRST FOLIO SIGNS OF WHEN VERBAL GAME PLAYING HAS TO STOP

1/ **non-embellished:** a section with neither capitals nor long spellings suggests that what is being discovered or spoken is so important to the character that there is no time to guss it up with vocal or mental excesses: an unusual moment of self-control

2/ **short sentence:** coming out of a society where debate was second nature, man y of Shakespeare's characters speak in long sentences in which ideas are stated, explored, redefined and summarized all before moving onto the next idea in the argument, discovery or debate: the longer sentence is the sign of a rhetorically trained mind used to public speaking (oratory), but at times an idea or discovery is so startling or inevitable that length is either unnecessary or impossible to maintain : hence the occasional very important short sentence suggests that there is no time for the niceties of oratorical adornment with which to sugar the pill - verbal games are at an end and now the basic core of the issue must be faced

3/ **monosyllabic:** with English being composed of two strands, the polysyllabic (stemming from French, Italian, Latin and Greek), and the monosyllabic (from the Anglo-Saxon), each strand has two distinct functions: the polysyllabic words are often used when there is time for fanciful elaboration and rich description (which could be described as 'excessive rhetoric') while the monosyllabic occur when, literally, there is no other way of putting a basic question or comment - Juliet's "Do you love me? I know thou wilt say aye" is a classic example of both monosyllables and non-embellishment: with monosyllables, only the naked truth is being spoken, nothing is hidden

Monologues from Shakespeare's First Folio for Women:
The Comedies

The Comedie of Errors

Adrianna

Patience unmov'd, no marvel though she pause,
2.1.32–41

Background: the married Adrianna is waiting with her unmarried sister Luciana to start the major meal of the day, dinner at noon. They cannot eat yet because, though it's way past the time Adrianna's highly social, philandering, husband should be home—he is still out drinking with his friends. Luciana has come up with a somewhat bookish approach to explaining the necessary relationship between the sexes. The following is the married Adrianna's practical direct experience reply to Luciana's rather apple-pie male-rightfully-dominating view of gender relationships.

Style: a speech, rather than dialogue, as part of a two-handed conversation

Where: in the home of Adrianna and the local Antipholus, who, unknown to anyone (including himself), is in fact the long lost infant twin for whom both his brother and Egeon are searching

To Whom: Luciana, her unmarried younger sister

# of Lines: 10

Probable Timing: 0.35 minutes

Take Note: With no capitals at all in the ten lines, this seems a very genuine cry from the 'deserted' Adrianna. The humour lies in the logic being confused, and long spellings suggesting her reactions are somewhat over the top—a very different response from the modern texts' jamming the two sentences together in one litany of never-ending complaint.

Adriana

1   Patience unmov'd! no marvel though she pause -
     They can be meek, that have no other cause :
     A wretched soul, bruis'd with adversity,
     We bid be quiet when we hear it cry ;
     But were we burd'ned with like weight of pain,
     As much, or more, we should our selves complain :
     So thou, that hast no unkind mate to grieve thee,
     With urging helpless patience would relieve me;
     But if thou live to see like right bereft,
     This fool -begg'd patience in thee will be left .

Adriana

1   Patience unmov'd, no marvel though she pause,
      They can be meeke, that have no other cause :
      A wretched soule bruis'd with adversitie,
      We bid be quiet when we heare it crie .

2   But were we burdned with like waight of paine,
      As much, or more, we should our selves complaine :
      So thou that hast no unkinde mate to greeve thee,
      With urging helpelesse patience would releeve me;
      But if thou live to see like right bereft,
      This foole-beg'd patience in thee will be left .

- yet despite the emotion (0/10), an argument of sorts is still being made: F's two sentences allow Adrianna to discount the general doctrine of the pain of a 'wretched soule, bruis'd in adversitie' especially when 'We' are not directly involved—a definite dig Luciana who is not (0/3 in F #1's four lines): this then allows the greater emotional impact (0/7 in six lines of F #2) of Adriana suggesting Luciana would not advise 'helplesse patience' if she had ever experienced what Adrianna is currently undergoing

- the (enforced?) quiet underscoring the two unembellished lines 'Patience unmov'd, no marvel though she pause' and 'But if thou live to see like right bereft' point to Adriana's deep exasperation with her 'theory'-smitten sister

The Comedie of Errors

Curtizan

Now out of doubt Antipholus is mad,
4.3.81–96

Background: despite the local Antipholus' suggestion that he would give an expensive chain to the Curtizan to spite Adrianna, he has only exchanged it for one of the Curtizan's rings. Indeed, he took her ring well in advance giving her the chain, which he's never taken possession of as it was given to his just-landed identical twin. Curtizan, believing as everyone else does that the visiting Antipholus is the local Antipholus, has demanded her ring back, which, of course, he has refused since he was not the one who took it. Having just been rejected by the visiting duo of Antipholus and Dromio, this is her only solo speech in the play.

Style: solo

Where: unspecified, but presumably some public space/street

To Whom: direct address to the audience

# of Lines: 16

Probable Timing: 0.50 minutes

Take Note: In a money-mad play, and with such a large sum at stake for the Curtizan ('fortie Duckets'), it's surprising so little emotional release is made throughout the speech and is almost matched intellectually (7/9 in sixteen lines). Thus, it would seem she is genuinely disturbed by the potential loss, and, in trying to work out what to do, she has little energy to waste .

Curtizan

1 Now out of doubt Antipholus is mad,
Else would he never so demean himself.

2 A ring he hath of mine worth forty ducats,
And for the same he promis'd me a chain:
Both one and other he denies me now .

3 The reason that I gather he is mad,
Besides this present instance of his rage,
Is a mad tale he told to day at dinner,
Of his own doors being shut against his entrance .

4 Belike his wife, acquainted with his fits,
On purpose shut the doors against his way .

5 My way is now to hie home to his house,
And tell his wife that, being lunatic,
He rush'd into my house, and took perforce
My ring away .

6   This course I fittest choose,
For forty ducats is too much to lose.

Curtizan

1   Now out of doubt Antipholus is mad,
     Else would he never so demeane himselfe,
     A Ring he hath of mine worth fortie Duckets,
     And for the same he promis'd me a Chaine,
     Both one and other he denies me now :
     The reason that I gather he is mad,
     Besides this present instance of his rage,
     Is a mad tale he told to day at dinner,
     Of his owne doores being shut against his entrance .

2   Belike his wife acquainted with his fits,
     On purpose shut the doores against his way :
     My way is now to hie home to his house,
     And tell his wife, that being Lunaticke,
     He rush'd into my house, and tooke perforce
     My Ring away .

3   This course I fittest choose,
     For fortie Duckets is too much to loose .

- thus, it is the occasional clusters of release that underscore her amazement that he would 'never so demeane himselfe'; plus 'Of his owne doores being shut', and the intellectual balance between 'Ring', 'Duckets' and 'Chaine'

- while the non-embellished lines point to where she is working hard to analyse the situation

  > "Both one and other he denies me now :/The reason that I gather he is mad,/Besides this present instance of his rage,/Is a mad tale he told to day at dinner,"

  > "My way is now to hie home to his house,/ and tell his wife,"

  > "He rush'd into my house,"

  plus the final

  > "This course I fittest choose,"

The Two Gentlemen of Verona

Julia

Nay, would I were so angred with the same :
1.2.101–126

Background: probably because she didn't want to satisfy the curiosity of her servant/companion Lucetta, Julia has ripped up unread a letter from her chosen sweetheart Protheus. Now Lucetta has left, Julia desperately wants to read what Protheus has written—the complicating factor is that the wind is blowing quite strongly. One note: the first line refers to the just ripped-up letter.

Style: solo

Where: somewhere outdoors, presumably in the garden of Julia's home

To Whom: herself, the ripped up letter, and the audience

# of Lines: 26

Probable Timing: 1.15 minutes

Take note: The opening onrush (F#1 being split into six by most modern texts) plus the enormous number of surround phrases, thirteen in all, five of which involve the emotional semicolon, are each testimony to the volcanic emotional underpinnings of the speech.

Julia

1   Nay, would I were so ang'red with the same .

2   O hateful hands, to tear such loving words !

3   Injurious wasps, to feed on such sweet honey,
     And kill the bees that yield it, with your stings .

4   I'll kiss each several paper, for amends .

5   Look, here is writ "kind Julia" .

6   Unkind Julia ,
     As in revenge of thy ingratitude,
     I throw thy name against the bruising stones,
     Trampling contemptuously on thy disdain .

7   And here is writ, "love wounded Protheus" .

8   Poor wounded name : my bosom as a bed
     Shall lodge thee till thy wound be throughly heal'd ;
     And thus I search it with a sovereign kiss .

9   But twice, or thrice, was "Protheus" written down :
     Be calm, good wind, blow not a word away,
     Till I have found each letter in the letter,
     Except mine own name ; that, some whirlwind bear
     Unto a ragged, fearful, hanging rock,
     And throw it thence into the raging sea .

10   Lo, here in one line is his name twice writ ,
     "Poor forlorn Protheus, passionate Protheus :
     To the sweet Julia"—that I'll tear away -
     And yet I will not, sith so prettily
     He couples it to his complaining names .

11   Thus will I fold them one upon another ;
     Now kiss, embrace, contend, do what you will .

Julia

1   Nay, would I were so angred with the same :
    Oh hatefull hands, to teare such loving words ;
    Injurious Waspes, to feede on such sweet hony,
    And kill the Bees that yeelde it, with your stings ;
    Ile kisse each severall paper, for amends :
    Looke, here is writ, kinde Julia : unkinde Julia ,
    As in revenge of thy ingratitude,
    I throw thy name against the bruzing-stones,
    Trampling contemptuously on thy disdaine .

2   And here is writ, *Love wounded Protheus* .

3   Poore wounded name : my bosome, as a bed,
    Shall lodge thee till thy wound be throughly heal'd ;
    And thus I search it with a soveraigne kisse .

4   But twice, or thrice, was *Protheus* written downe :
    Be calme (good winde) blow not a word away,
    Till I have found each letter, in the Letter,
    Except mine own name: That, some whirle-winde beare
    Unto a ragged, fearefull, hanging Rocke,
    And throw it thence into the raging Sea .

5   Loe, here in one line is his name twice writ :
    Poore forlorne Protheus, passionate Protheus :
    To the sweet Julia : that ile teare away :
    And yet I will not, sith so prettily
    He couples it, to his complaining Names ;
    Thus will I fold them, one upon another ;
    Now kisse, embrace, contend, doe what you will .

- it's not surprising that overall the releases are far more emotional than intellectual (14/29), though, interestingly, some mental recognition does come into play by the speech's end (5/16 in the thirteen lines of F #1-3, prior to the really intensive search for all the pieces of the ripped up letter; 9/13 in the thirteen lines of all that occurs thereafter)

- with so much opening emotion, it's not surprising that there are occasional wonderful vocally released clusters, such as

  "Oh hatefull hands, to teare such loving words ; /Injurious Waspes, to feede on such sweet hony,"

  and, once exploring the ripped up letter

  "Looke, here is writ, kinde Julia : unkinde Julia," therefore

  "That, some whirle-winde beare/Unto a ragged, fearefull, hanging Rocke,/ And throw it thence into the raging Sea."

- as noted above, the surround phrases clearly illuminate the different tensions she is undergoing, formed by both logical colons

  " . Nay, would I were so angred with the same :/Oh hatefull hands, to teare such loving words ; "
  " : Ile kisse each severall paper, for amends :/Looke, here is writ, kinde Julia : "
  " . But twice, or thrice, was Protheus written downe : "
  "Loe, here in one line is his name twice writ : /Poore forlorne Protheus, passionate Protheus : To the sweet Julia : that ile teare away : "

  and by, in this case, the more evocatively sensual semicolons

  " . Poore wounded name : my bosome, as a bed, /Shall lodge thee till thy wound be throughly heal'd ; /And thus I search it with a soveraigne kisse . "
  "He couples it, to his complaining Names ; /Thus will I fold them, one upon another ; /Now kisse, embrace, contend, doe what you will . "

The Two Gentlemen of Verona

Silvia

Oh Eglamoure, thou art a Gentleman :
4.3.11–36

Background: under the pressure of now doubly unwanted wooing, from the foolish Thurio whom her father is insisting she should marry, and the already betrothed-to-another-woman Protheus, Silvia is determined to leave Milan and journey to Mantua, where she believes her true-loveValentine to be. To achieve this she seeks the aid of the most honourable man she knows, Sir Eglamoure.

Style: speech as part of a two-handed scene

Where:: unspecified, somewhere in the palace

To Whom: Sir Eglamoure

# of Lines: 26

Probable Timing: 1.15 minutes

Take Note: In its opening sentence structure, F sets up a woman who initially is capable of making a precise argument, F #1 establishing Eglamoure's good qualities and a separate F #2 reminding him of the basic circumstances which afflict her—circumstances which then seem to become too much for her, for in the onrushed F #3 she jams together his doomed love experience and her own needs. Most modern texts reverse the process, allowing her to start with an onrush (mt. #1 = F #1-2), from which she then recovers (mt. #2-3 = F #3).

Silvia

1   O Eglamour, thou art a gentleman -
Think not I flatter, for I swear I do not -
Valiant, wise, remorsefull, well accomplish'd :
Thou art not ignorant what dear good will
I bear unto the banish'd Valentine,
Nor how my father would enforce me marry
Vain Thurio, whom my very soul [abhors] .

2   Thyself hast lov'd, and I have heard thee say
No grief did ever come so near thy heart,
As when thy lady and thy true love died,
Upon whose grave thou vow'dst pure chastity .

3   Sir Eglamour , I would to Valentine,
To Mantua, where I hear he makes abode ;
And for the ways are dangerous to pass,
I do desire thy worthy company,
Upon whose faith and honor I repose .

4   Urge not my father's anger,Eglamour,
But think upon my grief, a lady's grief,
And on the justice of my flying hence,
To keep me from a most unholy match,
Which heaven and fortune still rewards with plagues .

5   I do desire thee, even from a heart
As full of sorrows as the sea of sands,
To bear me company, and go with me,
If not, to hide what I have said to thee,
That I may venture to depart alone .

Silvia

1   Oh Eglamoure, thou art a Gentleman :
    Thinke not I flatter (for I sweare I doe not)
    Valiant, wise, remorse-full, well accomplish'd .

2   Thou art not ignorant what deere good will
    I beare unto the banish'd Valentine :
    Nor how my father would enforce me marry
    Vaine Thurio (whom my very soule [abhor'd].)

3   Thy selfe hast lov'd, and I have heard thee say
    No griefe did ever come so neere thy heart,
    As when thy Lady, and thy true-love dide,
    Upon whose Grave thou vow'dst pure chastitie :
    Sir Eglamoure : I would to Valentine
    To Mantua, where I heare, he makes aboad ;
    And for the waies are dangerous to passe,
    I doe desire thy worthy company,
    Upon whose faith and honor, I repose .

4   Urge not my fathers anger (Eglamoure)
    But thinke upon my griefe (a Ladies griefe)
    And on the justice of my flying hence,
    To keepe me from a most unholy match,
    Which heaven and fortune still rewards with plagues .

5   I doe desire thee, even from a heart
    As full of sorrowes, as the Sea of sands,
    To beare me company, and goe with me :
    If not, to hide what I have said to thee,
    That I may venture to depart alone .

- fascinatingly, whatever struggle she is undergoing, four of the five sentences end with non-embellished lines, as if after each exploration she is able to calm herself before continuing—a sense of necessary well-bred self-control perhaps?

- the quiet of some of the un-embellished phrases point to her belief in Eglamoure's goodness, regarding him as 'Valiant, wise, remorse-full, well accomplish'd', desiring the company of a man 'Upon whose faith and honor, I repose.', trusting him not to betray her if he decides not to help, 'If not, to hide what I have said to thee,/That I may venture to depart alone .'

- other non-embellished lines point to the strength of her moral convictions as regards joining Valentine ('And on the justice of my flying hence,') and avoiding an enforced marriage to Thurio ('Which heaven and fortune still rewards with plagues.')

- two surround phrases also underscore her need for Eglamoure's help—the opening ' . Oh Eglamoure, thou art a Gentleman : ' plus the very short and highly unusual ' : Sir Eglamoure : '; the latter could almost be a sigh or a momentary loss of thought

- while extending the surround phrase concept to a line and a half, the strength in speaking of her need is self-explanatory (' : I would to Valentine/To Mantua, where I heare, he makes aboad ; ')

- naturally the speech is highly emotional (12/27 overall), and, as befits such a bold step by a young woman, there are occasional fascinating bursts of emotional release, such as the praise of Eglamoure ('Thinke not I flatter (for I sweare I doe not)';), loathing for her father's choice of a husband ('Vaine Thurio (whom my very soule abhor'd)'), and her own anguish ('But thinke upon my griefe (a Ladies griefe)')

The Two Gentlemen of Verona

Julia

How many women would doe such a message ?
4.4.90–107

Background: Julia has disguised herself as a boy so as to travel unmolested to Milan, where, to her amazement and horror, her beloved and betrothed Protheus is actively wooing Silvia. To get close to him she offers herself as his servant, confident that her disguise as a boy will deceive him into failing to recognise her, as indeed it does. Unconsciously rubbing salt in her wounds, Protheus has ordered her as his new 'boy' to give a ring to Silvia (the giving of the ring being one of the most important parts of the traditional chivalric wooing/ betrothal ceremony): to make matters worse, the ring Protheus is planning on giving to Silvia is the very same ring Julia gave Protheus to mark their betrothal when they last saw each other in Verona!

Style: solo

Where: unspecified, somewhere in or near the palace

To Whom: direct audience address

# of Lines: 18

Probable Timing: 0.55 minutes

Take Note: The speech is a battle between passion (9/14 overall) and six separate moments of unembellished lines, suggesting that Julia is working very hard to find a balance between the two extremes of release and control.

Julia

1   How many women would do such a message ?

2   Alas, poor Protheus, thou hast entertain'd
    A fox to be the shepherd of thy lambs .
    Alas, poor fool, why do I pity him

3   That with his very heart despiseth me ?

4   Because he loves her, he despiseth me ;
    Because I love him, I must pity him .

5   This ring I gave him when he parted from me,
    To bind him to remember my good will ;
    And now am I (unhappy messenger)
    To plead for that which I would not obtain,
    To carry that which I would have refus'd ,
    To praise his faith which I would have disprais'd .

6   I am my master's true confirmed love;
    But cannot be true servant to my master,
    Unless I prove false traitor to myself .

7   Yet will I woo for him, but yet so coldly
    As, heaven it knows, I would not have him speed .

Julia

1   How many women would doe such a message ?

2   Alas poore Protheus, thou hast entertain'd
     A Foxe, to be the Shepheard of thy Lambs ;
     Alas, poore foole, why doe I pitty him
     That with his very heart despiseth me ?

3   Because he loves her, he despiseth me,
     Because I love him, I must pitty him .

4   This Ring I gave him, when he parted from me,
     To binde him to remember my good will :
     And now am I (unhappy Messenger)
     To plead for that, which I would not obtaine ;
     To carry that, which I would have refus'd ;
     To praise his faith, which I would have disprais'd .

5   I am my Masters true confirmed Love,
     But cannot be true servant to my Master,
     Unlesse I prove false traitor to my selfe .

6   Yet will I woe for him, but yet so coldly,
     As (heaven it knowes) I would not have him speed .

- the emotional content of the speech is underlined by the opening short sentence; the fact that three of the four pieces of major punctuation are semicolons; and the extra breath-thoughts (marked ,), especially the four in F #4, all of which point to the extra care with which she is exploring and expressing her fears

- the two surround phrases, both of which are heightened by being non-embellished and created by emotional semicolons, point to her dilemma in being asked to work against her own self-interest

    " ; To carry that, which I would have refus'd ; / To praise his faith, which I would have disprais'd . "

- the passion of her love-hate for Protheus gets most release in F #2 (4/7 in just three of the first four lines) only to be counterbalanced by the non-embellished lines that immediately follow, asking herself why should she pity Protheus

    "That with his very heart despiseth me ?/Because he loves her, he despiseth me, /Because I love him,…"

- and, in this sentence the first semicolon of the speech highlights even further her love hate for Protheus ' ;Alas, poore foole, why doe I pitty him '

- while the final non-embellishment heightens her monosyllabic passionate final wish 'I would not have him speed.'

The Two Gentlemen of Verona

Julia

A vertuous gentlewoman, milde, and beautifull .
4.4.180–205

Background: Silvia has granted only one of Protheus' requests, send-
ing him via Julia a picture of herself. With her own awkward self
analysis finished, and Silvia's comment before exiting, 'I weepe my
self to thinke upon thy words', Julia finally is alone on stage, and,
while speaking in praise of Silvia, compares herself as favourably as
she can with Silvia's picture.

Style: solo

Where: somewhere in or near the palace in Milan

To Whom: self and audience

# of Lines: 26

Probable Timing: 1.15 minutes

Take Note: F's onrushed middle of the speech (F #3-5) suggests a character in the throes of a self-examination far more awkward and ur-
gent than the modern texts show, most of which reset the three
sentences as seven.

Julia

1　A virtuous gentlewoman, mild and beautiful.

2　I hope my master's suit will be but cold,
　Since she respects my mistress' love so much .

3　Alas, how love can trifle with itself !

4　Here is her picture : let me see ; I think
　If I had such a tire, this face of mine
　Were full as lovely as is this of hers ;
　And yet the painter flatter'd her a little,
　Unless I flatter with myself too much .

5　Her hair is auburn, mine is perfect yellow :
　If that be all the difference in his love,
　I'll get me such a color'd periwig .

6　Her eyes are grey as glass, and so are mine ;
　Ay, but her forehead's low, and mine's as high .

7　What should it be that he respects in her,
　But I can make respective in myself,
　If this fond Love, were not a blinded god ?

8　Come, shadow, come, and take this shadow up,
　For 'tis thy rival .

9　　　　　　　O thou senseless form,
　Thou shalt be worshipp'd, kiss'd, lov'd, and ador'd ;
　And were there sense in his idolatry,
　My substance should be statue in thy stead .

10　I'll use thee kindly, for thy mistress' sake
　That us'd me so ; or else, by Jove, I vow,
　I should have scratch'd out your unseeing eyes,
　To make my master out of love with thee .

Julia

1 A vertuous gentlewoman, milde, and beautifull .

2 I hope my Masters suit will be but cold,
Since she respects my Mistris love so much .

3 Alas, how love can trifle with it selfe :
Here is her Picture : let me see, I thinke
If I had such a Tyre, this face of mine
Were full as lovely, as is this of hers ;
And yet the Painter flatter'd her a little,
Unlesse I flatter with my selfe too much .

4 Her haire is Aburne, mine is perfect Yellow ;
If that be all the difference in his love,
Ile get me such a coulour'd Perrywig :
Her eyes are grey as glasse, and so are mine :
I, but her fore-head's low, and mine's as high :
What should it be that he respects in her,
But I can make respective in my selfe ?
If this fond Love, were not a blinded god .

5 Come shadow, come, and take this shadow up,
For 'tis thy rivall : O thou sencelesse forme,
Thou shalt be worship'd, kiss'd, lov'd, and ador'd ;
And were there sence in his Idolatry,
My substance should be statue in thy stead .

6 Ile use thee kindly, for thy Mistris sake
That us'd me so : or else by Jove, I vow,
I should have scratch'd out your unseeing eyes,
To make my Master out of love with thee .

- the opening short sentence points to her amazement at liking her rival, which might go part way to explain the middle onrush of the speech, for the usual ploy of hating a rival cannot apply here

- the surround phrases highlight both her self-comparison with her rival's portrait

  " . Alas, how love can trifle with it selfe : /Here is her Picture : "

  " . Her haire is Aburne, mine is perfect Yellow ;"

  " : Her eyes are grey as glasse, and so are mine : "

  " : I, but her fore-head's low, and mine's as high : "

  and, extending the concept of a surround-phrase to a line and a half, to her no-way-out-of-the-dilemma-decision

  " . Come, shadow, come, and take this shadow up,/For 'tis thy rivall : "

  " . Ile use thee kindly, for thy Mistris sake/That us'd me so : "

- the non-embellished phrases set up the very contained realisations of not only her respect for Silvia

  "A vertuous gentlewoman,"

  and that hair colour seems to be the only real physical difference between them

  "If that be all the difference in his love, " especially since

  "I, but her fore-head's low, and mine's as high : "

  but also the key question that needs to be answered

  " What should it be that he respects in her,"

  followed by the sad realisation that

  "Thou shalt be worship'd, kiss'd, lov'd, and ador'd;/And were there sence in this… /My substance should be statue in thy stead."

- the constant struggle to find a plan of action can be seen in the swings of release from emotion about Silvia (F #1, 0/2), to the intellectual hope Protheus will not succeed in wooing her (F #2, 2/0), to a passionate yet still emotionally tinged examination of her rival (F #3-4, 7/11)

- and, while the inevitability of having to 'take this shadow up' (i.e her rival's picture) is passionate (2/3, F #5), so her decision to not damage the picture, respecting the earlier sympathetic treatment offered her by Silvia, is totally non-emotional (3/0, F #6)

Loves Labours Lost

Queene

Good L . Boyet, my beauty though but mean,
2.1.13–34

Background: because of the men's oath, the women cannot enter the palace grounds of Navar. The Princesse is mightily displeased from the moment they arrive, which of course affects the remainder of the male-female relationships throughout the rest of the play. In this, her first speech of the play, following an extravagant speech in her praise from Boyet, her chief counsellor cum chaperone, the Princesse charges Boyet in no uncertain terms to summon Navar so that they can get down to settling the business of land and money still outstanding between his father and hers, just as soon as possible.

Style: one on one address as part of at least a five handed scene

Where: unspecified, presumably outdoors somewhere near the palace

To Whom: directed toward counsellor/chaperone Boyet in front of her three Lady companions plus (possibly) some servants

# of Lines: 22

Probable Timing: 1.10 minutes

Take Note: Despite the annoyance of Boyet's flattery and the apparent snub from the Court of Navar, in this speech the Princesse/Queene does not resort to large-scale excesses (there aren't even any surround phrases in what follows). Instead, the sting of her rebukes, orders, and pointed comments are found in the non-embellished lines.

Princess

1   Good [Lord] Boyet, my beauty though but mean,
     Needs not the painted flourish of your praise :
     Beauty is bought by judgment of the eye,
     Not utt'red by base sale of chapmen's tongues .

2   I am less proud to hear you tell my worth
     [Than] you much willing to be counted wise
     In spending your wit in the praise of mine .

3   But now to task the tasker : good Boyet,
     You are not ignorant all-telling fame
     Doth noise abroad Navarre hath made a vow,
     Till painful study shall outwear three years
     No woman may approach his silent court ;
     Therefore to's seemeth it a needful course,
     Before we enter his forbidden gates,
     To know his pleasure; and in that behalf,
     Bold of your worthiness, we single you
     As our best-moving fair solicitor .

4   Tell him, the daughter of the King of France,
     On serious business craving quick dispatch,
     Importunes personal conference with his Grace .

5   Haste, signify so much, while we attend,
     Like humble -visag'd suitors, his high will .

Queene

1   Good [L.] Boyet, my beauty though but mean,
    Needs not the painted flourish of your praise :
    Beauty is bought by judgement of the eye,
    Not uttred by base sale of chapmens tongues :
    I am lesse proud to heare you tell my worth,
    [Then] you much willing to be counted wise,
    In spending your wit in the praise of mine .

2   But now to taske the tasker, good Boyet,
    You are not ignorant all-telling fame
    Doth noyse abroad Navar hath made a vow,
    Till painefull studie shall out-weare three yeares,
    No woman may approach his silent Court :
    Therefore to's seemeth it a needfull course,
    Before we enter his forbidden gates,
    To know his pleasure, and in that behalfe
    Bold of your worthinesse, we single you,
    As our best moving faire soliciter :
    Tell him, the daughter of the King of France,
    On serious businesse craving quicke dispatch,
    Importunes personall conference with his grace .

3   Haste, signifie so much while we attend,
    Like humble visag'd suters his high will .

- thus it's interesting that most of these calm lines are focused on Boyet

  "my beauty though but mean,/Needs not the painted flourish of your praise :"

  "Beauty is… /Not uttred by base sale of chapmens tongues:"

  "Than you much willing to be counted wise, /In spending your wit in the praise of mine ."

  then, dealing with Navar's refusal to allow the ladies admission to his palace

  "Before we enter his forbidden gates,/To know his pleasure,"

  and then back to dealing with Boyet once more

  "Haste, signifie so much while we attend,/Like humble visag'd suters hishigh will ."

- thus the opening dealing with Boyet is amazingly calm (just 1/3 in the seven lines of F #1, four of which are unembellished), but releases begin to appear as she turns to deal with the Navar situation

- first, there is a rare show of emotionally tinged passion as she (sarcastically?) lists the reason for women not being allowed to even 'approach his silent Court' (3/6 in the first six lines of F #2); but, after a non-embellished line and a half, this changes first to pure emotion as she selects Boyet (0/3), and then to passion once more as she describes what she wants him to do (the last three lines of F #2)

- and, having selected and briefed Boyet, so she finishes with an apparently quite easy non-embellished dismissal of him (F #3)

Loves Labours Lost

Rosaline

We are wise girles to mocke our Lovers so .
5.2.58–68

Background: the women seem to take the fact of the men having broken their oaths seriously, and, though they have been sent both poetry and gifts, are still determined to punish them as oath-breakers. Here Rosaline explains what she would like to do to Berowne. Two notes: the word 'pertaunt', line ten, has given rise to much discussion and alternative readings, 'the quarto's 'perttaunt-like' was long regarded as unintelligible and probably corrupt. Theobald read 'pedant-like', Hanmer 'portent-like', Capell 'pageant-like'; Dover Wilson (1923) adopted a suggestion of Moore Smith and read 'planet-like': in 1945, Percy Simpson offered a justification of the phrase on the grounds that 'paire-taunt' is the winning hand in an obsolete card game of 'Post and Pair', which presumably implies Rosaline will be able to beat whatever winning cards Berowne thinks he can play in their relationship: and the first line, marked {y}, is taken from an earlier speech by the Princess.

Style: as part of a five handed scene

Where: wherever the French Ladies private encampment is

To Whom: the three young Frenchwomen and Boyet

# of Lines: 11

Probable Timing: 0.40 minutes

Take Note: F's ungrammatical structure undermines Rosaline's apparent ease.

13/ **Rosaline**

1 {†} We are wise girls to mock our lovers so .

2   They are worse fools to purchase mocking so .

3   That same Berowne I'll torture ere I go .

4   O that I knew he were but in by th'week!

5   How I would make him fawn, and beg, and seek,
    And wait the season, and observe the times,
    And spend his prodigal wits in bootless rhymes,
    And shape his service wholly to my hests,
    And make him proud to make me proud that jests !

6   So [pair-taunt] like would I oe'rsway his state
    That he should be my fool and I his fate .

Rosaline

1 {†} We are wise girles to mocke our Lovers so .

2   They are worse fooles to purchase mocking so .

3   That same Berowne ile torture ere I goe .

4   O that I knew he were but in by th'weeke,
How I would make him fawne, and begge, and seeke,
And wait the season, and observe the times,
And spend his prodigall wits in booteles rimes .

5   And shape his service wholly to my device,
And make him proud to make me proud that jests .

6   So [pertaunt] like would I o'resway his state,
That he shold be my foole, and I his fate .

- not only does the speech start rather more emotionally than intellectually (2/4, F #1-3), the fact that is starts with three short sentences shows just how much Rosaline is revealing herself, quickly moving from idea to idea without unnecessary elaboration

- though most modern texts set a rational single line sentence (mt. #4) expressing the hope that Berowne is trapped (the contemporary meaning of 'in by the weeke'), F's onrushed ungrammatical fast-link connection (via a comma) to what follows clearly shows a somewhat enthusiastic and uncontrolled Rosaline on an imaginative roll

- and the emotional listing of what Rosaline would like to put Berowne through (F #4, 0/6) also ends ungrammatically (according to modern texts) with a period: yet intellectually F's period is splendid, for it allows her a moment before going on via a new sentence to sum up, and this new sentence is orthographically enhanced by being completely unembellished, as if the thought almost takes her breath away

Loves Labours Lost
Queene

A time me thinkes too short,
5.2.788–812

Background: as the joviality surrounding the presentation of 'The Nine Worthies' peaks, a figure dressed in black arrives to announce the death of the Princesse's father the King of France. As Boyet and she realise, now Queene rather than Princesse, she and her train must leave immediately. Both Navar (awkwardly) and Berowne (much more succinctly) try to express their true feelings so as to get some indication in return from the four French women as to how they regard the men who have professed their love. The following is the Princesse/ Queene's no holds barred response to Navar's (finally) plain-speaking request, 'Now at the latest minute of the houre/Grant us your loves.'

Style: one on one, probably with six others overhearing

Where: somewhere near either the palace or the French Ladies' encampment, amidst the detritus left behind by the players

To Whom: Ferdinand of Navar, in front of the three other would-be couples, Berowne-Rosaline, Longavile-Maria, Dumaine-Katherine

# of Lines: 25

Probable Timing: 1.15 minutes

Take note: With so much having just occurred, the announcement of the death of her father, her resultant accession as Queene of France, and Ferdinand's last minute proposal, it's not surprising that F shows the speech as a struggle between self-control via trying to remain calm (five and a half unembellished lines) and emotion.

Queene

1   A time [methinks] too short
To make a world-without-end bargain in .

2   No, no, my lord, your Grace is perjur'd much,
Full of dear guiltiness, and therefore this :
If for my love (as there is no such cause)
You will do aught, this shall you do for me :
Your oath I will not trust, but go with speed
To some forlorn and naked hermitage,
Remote from all the pleasures of the world ;
There stay until the twelve celestial signs
Have brought about their annual reckoning .

3   If this austere insociable life,
Change not your offer made in heat of blood ;
If frosts and fasts, hard lodging, and thin weeds
Nip not the gaudy blossoms of your love
But that it bear this trial, and last love ;
Then at the expiration of the year,
Come challenge me, challenge me by these deserts,
And by this virgin palm now kissing thine,
I will be thine ; and till that instant shut
My woeful self up in a mourning house,
Raining the tears of lamentation
For the remembrance of my father's death .

4   If this thou do deny, let our hands part,
Neither intitled in the other's heart .

Queene

1　A time [me thinkes] too short,
　　To make a world-without-end bargaine in ;
　　No, no my Lord, your Grace is perjur'd much,
　　Full of deare guiltinesse, and therefore this :
　　If for my Love (as there is no such cause)
　　You will do ought, this shall you do for me .

2　Your oth I will not trust : but go with speed
　　To some forlorne and naked Hermitage,
　　Remote from all the pleasures of the world :
　　There stay, untill the twelve Celestiall Signes
　　Have brought about their annuall reckoning .

3　If this austere insociable life,
　　Change not your offer made in heate of blood :
　　If frosts, and fasts, hard lodging, and thin weeds
　　Nip not the gaudie blossomes of your Love,
　　But that it beare this triall, and last love :
　　Then at the expiration of the yeare,
　　Come challenge me, challenge me by these deserts,
　　And by this Virgin palme, now kissing thine,
　　I will be thine : and till that instant shut
　　My wofull selfe up in a mourning house,
　　Raining the teares of lamentation,
　　For the remembrance of my Fathers death .

4　If this thou do denie, let our hands part,
　　Neither intitled in the others hart .

- with the overall emotional imbalance (9/18) , at no time does she succeed in retaining intellectual control: the closest she comes is the passionate denunciation of Ferdinand for being 'perjur'd much' (2/2)—though the ensuing adjective seems to suggest that she not only understands but might actually approve of his love ('deare guilt-inesse')—and the subsequent emotionally tingged passionate challenge that he go into retreat for twelve months (4/5 to the end of F #2)

- the unembellished lines (not in order) show her mind at its clearest

  "You will do ought, this shall you do for me ."

  "If this austere insociable life,/Change not your offer…"

  "Come challenge me, challenge me by these deserts,"

  "If this thou do denie, let our hands part,/Neither intitled in the others hart ."

  and especially the unembellished monosyllabic surround phrase '. Your oth I will not trust : '

- F #3's three extra breath-thoughts all point to key moments where the Princesse/Queene needs an extra thought for clarification or breath for self-control as she anticipates the pain she will have to endure over the next twelve months

- rejecting the timing of and time-line inherent in Ferdinand's proposal, F #1's first two lines start emotionally, heightened by line two ending with a semicolon (0/2); then comes F #1-2's mi of unembellished lines and passion as discussed above

- her determined elaboration in F #3 that this is the only way to win her is emotional once again (3/9)

- and it is a tribute to her sense of self that the speech ends completely unembellished (0/0, F #4), though the short spelling of 'denie' and 'hart' suggest she is struggling hard to hold herself in check (restraining from tears perhaps)

A Midsommer Nights Dreame

Hermia

**My good Lysander,/
I sweare to thee, by Cupids strongest bow,**
1.1.168–178

Background: this is Hermia's enthusiastic response to Lysander's urgings that they run away from Athens

Style: part of a two-handed scene, essentially self-explanatory

Where: somewhere in Theseus' palace where the confrontation has just ended

To Whom: her beloved Lysander

# of Lines: 11

Probable Timing: 0.40 minutes

Hermia

1   My good Lysander,
I swear to thee, by Cupids strongest bow,
By his best arrow with the golden head,
By the simplicity of Venus' Doves,
By that which knitteth souls and prospers [loves],
And by that fire which burn'd the Carthage queen,
When the false Troyan under sail was seen,
By all the vows that ever men have broke,
(In number more [than] ever women spoke)
In that same place thou hast appointed me
To-morrow truly will I meet with thee .

Hermia

1   My good Lysander,
    I sweare to thee, by Cupids strongest bow,
    By his best arrow with the golden head,
    By the simplicitie of Venus Doves,
    By that which knitteth soules, and prospers [love],
    And by that fire which burn'd the Carthage Queene,
    When the false Troyan under saile was seene,
    By all the vowes that ever men have broke,
    (In number more [then] ever women spoke)
    In that same place thou hast appointed me,
    To morrow truly will I meete with thee .

- given the circumstances, the onrushed single line sentence is only to be expected, as is the fact that Hermia starts out strongly intellectually (7/3 in the first five and a half lines), calling upon classical allusions for support (a traditional Elizabethan rhetorical device) and providing most of the capitals

- what may be surprising is that before her agreement comes a three line attack on deceitful men ('false Troyan' etc.), the first two of which start out emotionally (0/4) and then, quite fascinatingly, comes an unembellished line, also concentrating on all men's deceptions 'In number more [then] ever women spoke' (is this one of her greatest fears? and does this affect her in the 'two men pursuing Helena sequence' later in the play?)

- and the big step of agreeing to run away remains unembellished though, given what has just been said, the calm may be more than just an awareness of the enormity of what they are about to do

    "In that same place thou hast appointed me/To morrow truly…"

A Midsommer Nights Dreame

Helena

Cal you me faire ? that faire againe unsay,

1.1.181–193

Background: this is Helena's first sequence in the play, triggered by
Hermia's greeting 'God speede faire Helena, whither away?'. With
the knowledge that her one-time boyfriend Demetrius has abandoned her to pursue Hermia, even though Hermia loves and is
loved by Lysander, the speech is self-explanatory.

Style: essentially a woman to woman address, as part of a three-handed scene

Where: somewhere in Theseus' palace, where the confrontation with
Egeus has just ended

To Whom: Hermia, with Lysander in attendance

# of Lines: 13

Probable Timing: 0.45 minutes

Take Note: There is a great difference between the sentence structures
of the two texts, for while the modern texts set a somewhat rational
well balanced eight sentence argument, the two sentence F structure
suggests a much more uncontrolled release, at least until the end.

Helena

1   Call you me fair ?

2   That fair again unsay .

3   Demetrius loves [your] fair .

4   O happy fair !

5   Your eyes are lodestars, and your tongues sweet air
     More tuneable [than] lark to shepherd's ear
     When wheat is green, when hawthorn buds appear.

6   Sickness is catching ; O, were favor so,
     [Yours would] I catch, fair Hermia, ere I go ;
     My ear should catch your voice, my eye, your eye,
     My tongue should catch your tongue's sweet melody.

7   Were the world mine, Demetrius being bated,
     The rest I'll give to be to you translated .

8   O, teach me how you look, and with what art
     You sway the motion of Demetrius' heart .

Helena

1   Cal you me faire ? that faire againe unsay,
     Demetrius loves[you] faire : O happie faire !
     Your eyes are loadstarres, and your tongues sweet ayre
     More tuneable [then] Larke to shepheards eare,
     When wheate is greene, when hauthorne buds appeare,
     Sicknesse is catching : O were favor so,
     [Your words] I catch, faire Hermia ere I go,
     My eare should catch your voice, my eye, your eye,
     My tongue should catch your tongues sweet melodie,
     Were the world mine, Demetrius being bated,
     The rest Ile give to be to you translated .

2   O teach me how you looke, and with what art
     You sway the motion of Demetrius hart .

- quite remarkably, the huge onrushed F #1 splits in two orthographically, a very emotional (overwrought? melodramatic?) start (2/15 in the first five and a half lines), and a finish only occasionally intellectual or emotional (3/3 in the final seven and a half)

- the split occurs once Helena comes up with the idea that, if only she could imitate Hermia's behaviour, she might yet win back Demetrius, for at this moment nearly all the earlier emotion disappears

- thus, while the much calmer second part of F #1 might be directed towards Hermia and Demetrius, it may also be inner directed (perhaps a dream of what could/might be, if only...)

A Midsommer Nights Dreame

Queene

Set your heart at rest,/
The Fairy land buyes not the childe of me,
2.1.121–137

Background: in response to the deeply felt chaos expressed in her previ-
ous speech , Oberon offers a truce if only she will surrender to him the
Indian Boy (the root of their more than year-long quarrel) to be his
'Henchman', a bargain that she emphatically refuses.

Style: one on one address in front of an unspecified number of others

Where: somewhere in the woods

To Whom: Oberon, in front of both their trains including the Fairie
and Pucke who were talking earlier

# of Lines: 17

Probable Timing: 0.55 minutes

Take note: Though still deeply emotionally affected, here Titania offers far less logic and intellect than in her prior speech

Queene

1   Set your heart at rest ;
     The fairy land buys not the child of me .

2   His mother was a vot'ress of my order,
     And in the spiced Indian air, by night,
     Full often hath she gossip'd by my side,
     And sat with me on Neptune's yellow sands,
     Marking th'embarked traders on the flood ;
     When we have laugh'd to see the sails conceive
     And grow big-bellied with the wanton wind ;
     Which she, with pretty and with swimming [gait],
     Following (her womb then rich with my young squire)
     Would imitate, and sail upon the land
     To fetch me trifles, and return again,
     As from a voyage, rich with merchandise .

3   But she, being mortal, of that boy did die,
     And for her sake [do I] rear up her boy ;
     And for her sake I will not part with him .

Queene

1 Set your heart at rest,
    The Fairy land buyes not the childe of me,
    His mother was a Votresse of my Order,
    And in the spiced Indian aire, by night
    Full often hath she gossipt by my side,
    And sat with me on Neptunes yellow sands,
    Marking th'embarked traders on the flood,
    When we have laught to see the sailes conceive,
    And grow big bellied with the wanton winde :
    Which she with pretty and with swimming [gate],
    Following (her wombe then rich with my yong squire)
    Would imitate, and saile upon the Land,
    To fetch me trifles, and returne againe,
    As from a voyage, rich with merchandize .

2 But she being mortall, of that boy did die,
    And for her sake [I doe] reare up her boy,
    And for her sake I will not part with him .

- the fact that Titania's opening emotion is matched by her intellect (5/6 in F #1's first nine lines), especially when balanced against the final emotion of the speech, is great proof of how much she needs to have all present (Oberon especially) understand the factual base of her refusal

- yet F #1's onrush, with the introduction of the all important explanation of who the Boy's mother was springing forth via a non-grammatical fast-link comma after the first two lines, gives the clue to her still unbalanced state

- as the good times of her Votresse's pregnancy are so lovingly described, emotion takes over (1/5 in the last five lines of F #1)

- the description of her death is equally emotional (0/3 in the first two lines of F #2)

- and the refusal to hand over the boy is icily calm in its monosyllabic unembellished finality 'And for her sake I will not part with him.', matching the equally icy opening 'Set your heart at rest,'

A Midsommer Nights Dreame

Helena

O I am out of breath, in this fond chace,
2.2.88–102

Background: though Demetrius ran away from her as threatened, the still very game Helena pursued him and caught up with him, only to be almost immediately abandoned again, his last words warning 'Stay on thy perill, I alone will goe'. The following is her response, and discovery.

Style: solo, until F #7/mt. #8

Where: somewhere in the woods

To Whom: direct audience address, and then the sleeping/potion zapped Lysander

# of Lines: 15

Probable Timing: 0.50 minutes

Take note: It seems that the opening words are very true and she really is out of breath, in that save for the single proper name 'Hermia', the first four and half lines (F #1-2) show no release and, thus un-embellished, offer a very quiet opening (probably more exhausted and despairing than calm).

Helena

1 O, I am out of breath, in this fond chase!

2 The more my prayer, the lesser is my grace .

3 Happy is Hermia, whereso'er she lies,
   For she hath blessed and attractive eyes .

4 How came her eyes so bright ?

5   Not with salt tears;
   If so, my eyes are oft'ner wash'd [than] hers .

6 No, no, I am as ugly as a bear ;
   For beasts that meet me run away for fear.

7 Therefore no marvel though Demetrius
   Do, as a monster, fly my presence thus .

8 What wicked and dissembling glass of mine
   Made me compare with Hermia's sphery eyne !

9 But who is here ?

10   Lysander ! on the ground ?

11 Dead, or asleep ?

12   I see no blood, no wound .

13 Lysander, if you live, good sir, awake .

Helena

1   O I am out of breath, in this fond chace,
    The more my prayer, the lesser is my grace,
    Happy is Hermia, wheresoere she lies ;
    For she hath blessed and attractive eyes .

2   How came her eyes so bright ?

3   Not with salt teares .

4   If so, my eyes are oftner washt [then] hers .

5   No, no, I am as ugly as a Beare ;
    For beasts that meete me, runne away for feare,
    Therefore no marvaile, though Demetrius
    Doe as a monster, flie my presence thus .

6   What wicked and dissembling glasse of mine,
    Made me compare with Hermias sphery eyne ?

7   But who is here ?

8   Lysander on the ground ;
    Deade or asleepe ?

9   I see no bloud, no wound,
    Lysander, if you live, good sir awake .

- but as Helena slowly recovers and begins to focus yet again on her own inadequacies as compared to Hermia, the depths of feeling in this unflattering comparison can be seen in that the three sentences of F #2-4 are all short, one (#2) unembellished and monosyllabic, and a second (#4) unembellished

- and in the comparison her emotions are released once more (0/9, F #3-6)

- while the discovery of Lysander forces her back to some semblance of restrained self-control (0/2, F #7-9)

- even in the supposedly controlled moments, the semicolons show that emotions still bubble underneath, first about Hermia's beauty

  " ; For she hath blessed and attractive eyes . "

  and then in the apparently calm discovery of Lysander

  " . Lysander on the ground ; /Deade or asleepe ? "

A Midsommer Nights Dreame

Hermia

Helpe me Lysander, helpe me ; do thy best
2.2.145–156

Background: not knowing that the now enchanted/love potion zapped Lysander has deliberately left her to embark on his new chivalric and knightly quest to woo Helena, Hermia awakes from a bad dream, as she eventually discovers, alone.

Style: though in fact solo, initially to a supposedly present partner

Where: in the woods

To Whom: the absent Lysander

# of Lines: 12

Probable Timing: 0.40 minutes

Take Note: The onrush of F #3 and F #7 allows Hermia a much more understandable, faster release and/or dismissal of her fear than most modern texts (which split the text into two and three sentences, respectively).

Hermia

1   Help me, Lysander, help me ! do thy best
    To pluck this crawling serpent from my breast !

2   Ay me, for pity! what a dream was here!

3   Lysander, look how I do quake with fear .

4   Methought a serpent eat my heart away,
    And [you] sat smiling at his cruel prey .

5   Lysander ! what remov'd ?

6   Lysander !, lord !
    What, out of hearing gone ?

7   No sound, no word ?

8   Alack, where are you ?

9   Speak, and if you hear ;
    Speak, of all loves !

10   I [swoon] almost with fear .

11 No ? then I well perceive you are not nigh:
    Either death, or you, I'll find immediately

Hermia

1   Helpe me Lysander, helpe me ; do thy best
    To plucke this crawling serpent from my brest .

2   Aye me, for pitty ; what a dreame was here ?

3   Lysander looke, how I do quake with feare :
    Me-thought a serpent eate my heart away,
    And [yet] sat smiling at his cruell prey .

4   Lysander, what remoov'd ?

5   Lysander, Lord,
    What, out of hearing, gone ?

6   No sound, no word ?

7   Alacke where are you ? speake and if you heare :
    Speake of all loves ; I [sound] almost with feare .

8   No, then I well perceive you are not nye,
    Either death or you Ile finde immediately .

- that six of the seven surround phrases are formed in part by emotional semicolons goes a long way to underscore how emotional she really is

  " . Helpe me Lysander, helpe me ; do thy best/To plucke this crawling serpent from my brest . /Aye me, for pitty ; what a dreame was here ? "

  " : Speake of all loves ; I [sound] almost with feare . "

  as does her logical (colon created surround phrase) self-assessment

  " . Lysander looke, how I do quake with feare : "

- while the non-embellished phrases speak to her fear of being left alone

  " . What, out of hearing, gone? No sound, no word?"

  with the quiet being either non-energised fear, or, more in the heroine-type genre, a deliberately self-enforced calm

- not surprisingly, the speech is emotional throughout (2/18 overall)

A Midsommer Nights Dreame

Titania

Out of this wood, do not desire to goe,
between 3.1.152–174

Background: the love potion zapped Titania is awoken by the singing of the just transformed-into-an-Asse Bottome, and the full force of Oberon's magic potion hits straightaway. In this speech, despite Titania's obvious charms, Bottome has expressed the desire to 'get out of this wood', something Titania will not allow.

Style: as part of a two-handed scene

Where: Titania's bower

To Whom: the just transformed-into-an-Asse Bottome

# of Lines: 22

Probable Timing: 1.10 minutes

Titania

1   Out of this wood do not desire to go;
    Thou shalt remain here, whether thou wilt or no .

2   I am a spirit of no common rate ;
    The summer still doth tend upon my state ;
    And I do love thee ; therefore go with me .

3   I'll give thee fairies to attend on thee ;
    And they shall fetch thee jewels from the deep,
    And sing, while thou on pressed flowers dost sleep .

4   And I will purge thy mortal grossness so,
    That thou shalt like an aery spirit go .

---

5   Peaseblossom! Cobweb! Moth! Mustardseed!

---

6   Be kind and courteous to this gentleman,
    Hop in his walks and gambol in his eyes;
    Feed him with apricocks, and dewberries,
    With purple grapes, green figs, and mulberries;
    The honeybags steal from the humble- bees,
    And for night-tapers crop their waxen thighs,
    And light them at the fiery glow-worm's eyes,
    To have my love to bed, and to arise ;
    And pluck the wings from painted butterflies,
    To fan the moonbeams from his sleeping eyes .

7   Nod to him, elves, and do him courtesies .

Titania

1   Out of this wood, do not desire to goe,
     Thou shalt remaine here, whether thou wilt or no .

2   I am a spirit of no common rate :
     The Summer still doth tend upon my state,
     And I doe love thee ; therefore goe with me,
     Ile give thee Fairies to attend on thee ;
     And they shall fetch thee Jewels from the deepe,
     And sing, while thou on pressed flowers dost sleepe :
     And I will purge thy mortall grossenesse so,
     That thou shalt like an airie spirit go .

---

3   Pease-blossome, Cobweb, Moth, Mustard-seede

---

4   Be kinde and curteous to this Gentleman,
     Hop in his walkes, and gambole in his eies,
     Feede him with Apricocks, and Dewberries,
     With purple Grapes, greene Figs, and Mulberries,
     The honie-bags steale from the humble Bees,
     And for night-tapers crop their waxen thighes,
     And light them at the fierie-Glow-wormes eyes,
     To have my love to bed, and to arise :
     And plucke the wings from painted Butterflies,
     To fan the Moone-beames from his sleeping eies .

5   Nod to him Elves, and doe him curtesies .

- the surround phrases seem to reinfoce her physical awareness, first as noted in the previous speech

    " . I am a spirit of no common rate : "

  especially the second, created by the emotional semicolons

    " ; therefore goe with me,/Ile give thee Fairies to atend on thee ; "

- the onrushed F #2 suggests that the bribery comes out in one long gush, much more understandable than the rather calculating stepping stones the modern texts have created by splitting F #2 in three

- not surprisingly, the speech starts out emotionally (2/8, F #1-2), which, after the calling in of her retinue (F #3), continues momentarily for the first two lines of instruction opening F #4 (1/3)

- the proposed feeding of him, the next three lines, becomes quite intellectual (6/3) as she spells out exactly what food (aphrodisiacs perhaps?) she wants (6/3), while the two-line order to prepare torches for the bedroom becomes somewhat emotional (1/2)

- however, the thought of 'To have my love to bed, and to arise' drives her into a momentary unembellished reverie, though whether quite calm or her breath being taken by the image is up to each actress to decide

- from which she recovers quite quickly, for the last two (sybaritic) lines of F #4 and F #5's final short line order become passionate (3/4)

A Midsommer Nights Dreame

Helena

O spight ! O hell ! I see you are all bent
3.2.145–161

Background: since both the zapped/love-potioned Lysander and
Demetrius are wooing her so extravagantly, and even though
Demetrius is saying everything she has longed to hear (calling her
'goddesse, nimph, perfect, divine'), Helena highly doubts their sin-
cerity—as she tells them in no uncertain terms.

Style: as part of a three-handed scene

Where: somewhere in the woods

To Whom: to the love potion zapped Lysander and Demetrius

# of Lines: 17

Probable Timing: 0.55 minutes

Take Note: Here there seems to be a fine struggle between control
and emotion, emphasised by the most unusual setting of, for F, two
extraordinarily rare exclamation marks (at the end of F #1 & #2),
and the fact that the speech starts with two very short sentences.

Helena

1   O spite !

2   O hell !

3   I see you [all are] bent
     To set against me, for your merriment .

4   If you were civil and knew courtesy,
     You would not do me thus much injury .

5   Can you not hate me, as I know you do,
     But you must join in souls to mock me too ?

6   If you [were] men, as men you are in show,
     You would not use a gentle lady so ;
     To vow, and swear, and superpraise my parts,
     When I am sure you hate me with your hearts .

7   You both are rivals, and love Hermia ;
     And now both rivals, to mock Helena .

8   A trim exploit, a manly enterprise,
     To conjure tears up in a poor maid's eyes
     With your derision !

9   None of noble sort
     Would so offend a virgin, and extort
     A poor soul's patience, all to make you sport .

Helena

1   O spight !

2   O hell !

3   I see you [are all] bent
     To set against me, for your merriment :
     If you were civill, and knew curtesie,
     You would not doe me thus much injury .

4   Can you not hate me, as I know you doe,
     But you must joyne in soules to mocke me to ?

5   If you [are] men, as men you are in show,
     You would not use a gentle Lady so ;
     To vow, and sweare, and superpraise my parts,
     When I am sure you hate me with your hearts .

6   You both are Rivals, and love Hermia ;
     And now both Rivals to mocke Helena .

7   A trim exploit, a manly enterprize,
     To conjure teares up in a poore maids eyes,
     With your derision ; none of noble sort,
     Would so offend a Virgin, and extort
     A poore soules patience, all to make you sport .

- right from the start, the clash between the exclamation points of F #1-2 (indicating unusually excessive release) and the attempted control shown in the two and a half unembellished lines in the opening four lines of F #1-3 shows the extremes she is undergoing (the demands of social politeness and personal need clashing perhaps)

- the two onrushed sentences (F #3 and F #7) also show where the rational character created by modern texts (which split both F sentences in two) cracks a little in her hurt accusation of the men not being 'civill' (F #3) and not being of 'noble sort' (F #7)

- the three semicolons (F #5, #6, #7) all relate to moments of her belief in their mistreatment of her

  "You would not use a gentle Lady so;"

  plus the surround phrases

  " . You both are Rivals, and love Hermia ; /And now both Rivals to mocke Helena . "

  with the final summation

  " ; none of noble sort/Would so offend a Virgin,…"

- despite the struggles, the speech opens under a fair degree of control (0/2 in the first four lines, F #1-3), then becomes much more emotional (0/4, F #4) as she accuses them of mocking her

- then, though mental discipline momentarily takes over as her stripping them down intensifies (5/2, F #5-6), it cannot last, and her emotions come to the fore once more in the final, onrushed, F #7 (1/5)

The Merchant of Venice

Jessica

I am sorry thou wilt leave my Father so,
between 2.3.1–21

Background: this is the first speech in the play for Shylocke's daughter: as such it is self-explanatory.

Style: as part of a two-handed scene

Where: somewhere in Shylocke's home

To Whom: Launcelet, who is leaving Shylocke's employment to become a member of Bassanio's entourage

# of Lines: 15

Probable Timing: 0.50 minutes

Take Note: The modern texts create for their Jessica a very precise rational eight sentence farewell, while F's Jessica has a two sentence speech full of ungrammatical links, redolent both of urgency and fear of discovery.

Jessica

1   I am sorry thou wilt leave my father so .

2   Our house is hell, and thou, a merry devil,
     Did'st rob it of some taste of tediousness .

3   But fare thee well, there is ducat for thee,
     And, Lancelot, soon at supper shalt thou see
     Lorenzo, who is thy new master's guest .

4   Give him this letter, do it secretly,
     And so farewell .

5   I would not have my father
     See me [in] talk with thee .

---

6   Alack, what heinous sin is it in me
     To be ashamed to be my Fathers child!

7   But though I am a daughter to his blood,
     I am not to his manners .

8   O Lorenzo,
     If thou keep promise, I shall end this strife,
     Become a Christian and thy loving wife .

Jessica

1   I am sorry thou wilt leave my Father so,
Our house is hell, and thou a merrie divell
Did'st rob it of some taste of tediousnesse ;
But far thee well, there is ducat for thee,
And Lancelet, soone at supper shalt thou see
Lorenzo, who is thy new Maisters guest,
Give him this Letter, doe it secretly,
And so farwell : I would not have my Father
See me [ ] talke with thee .

---

2   Alacke, what hainous sinne is it in me
To be ashamed to be my Fathers childe,
But though I am a daughter to his blood,
I am not to his manners : O Lorenzo,
If thou keepe promise I shall end this strife,
Become a Christian, and thy loving wife .

- that Jessica is rushed is clearly seen in the first long F sentence (which modern texts split into five rational separate statements) where the end of lines 1 and 6 are joined to the next simply by onrolling quick-link commas, whereas modern texts have replaced them with periods: this device is also seen at the end of line two of F sentence #2, and in all three cases the F setting suggests an immediacy not maintained by the modern texts

- the single surround phrase in the speech explains just why the F Jessica is so rushed

  " : I would not have my Father/See me talke with thee . "

- though there are the same number of capitals as long spellings (9/9), each come in clusters: there seems to be a three way struggle within her: sometimes her emotions get the better of her, as with the first two lines of F sentence #2, dealing with her disloyalty to her father (0/3); sometimes she can establish personal self control with no embellishment, as she does with the decision to reject her father in the next line and a half, and the passion of both head and heart sometimes are given sway, as with the plotting to get a message to Lorenzo, in the last five lines of sentence #1 (5/5)

The Merchant of Venice

Portia

I pray you tarrie, pause a day or two
3.2.1–24

Background: this is the first face-to-face speech and scene between the mutually smitten Portia and Bassanio. As her rather awkward attempt to prevent him from making a casket choice just yet (for if he makes the wrong choice, by terms of her father's will he must never see Portia again), it is self-explanatory.

Style: one on one, in front of a small group

Where: near or in the casket-room

To Whom: Bassanio, in front of Gratiano and Nerrissa, perhaps some of Portia's household, including musicians

# of Lines: 24

Probable Timing: 1.10 minutes

Take Note: The modern text's ten sentences present a Portia much more in control than the 4 sentence Folio (matched exactly by the quarto). Also, F's setting of three semicolons as opposed to just two colons (two of the three coming in the extended first sentence) suggests that Portia's F inner volcano is much more difficult to control than that of her modern counterpart.

Portia

1   I pray you tarry, pause a day or two
Before you hazard, for in choosing wrong
I lose your company ; therefore forbear a while .

2   There's something tells me (but it is not love)
I would not lose you, and you know yourself,
Hate counsels not in such a quality .

3   But lest you should not understand me well -
And yet a maiden hath no tongue, but thought -
I would detain you here some month or two
Before you venture for me .

4   I could teach you
How to choose right, but then I am forsworn.

5   So will I never be, so may you miss me,
But if you do, you'll make me wish a sin,
That I had been forsworn.

6   Beshrow your eyes,
They have o'erlook'd me and divided me :
One half of me is yours, the other half yours -
Mine own, I would say ; but [if] mine, then yours,
And so all yours .

7   O, these naughty times
Puts bars between the owners and their rights !

8   And so though yours, not yours .

9   Prove it so,
Let fortune go to hell for it, not I .

10   I speak too long, but 'tis to piece the time,
To [eche] it, and to draw it out in length,
To stay you from election .

Portia

1   I pray you tarrie, pause a day or two
      Before you hazard, for in choosing wrong
      I loose your companie ; therefore forbeare a while,
      There's something tels me (but it is not love)
      I would not loose you, and you know your selfe,
      Hate counsailes not in such a quallitie ;
      But least you should not understand me well,
      And yet a maiden hath no tongue, but thought,
      I would detaine you here some month or two
      Before you venture for me .

2   I could teach you
      How to choose right, but then I am forsworne,
      So will I never be, so may you misse me,
      But if you doe, youle make me wish a sinne,
      That I had beene forsworne : Beshrow your eyes,
      They have ore-lookt me and devided me,
      One halfe of me is yours, the other halfe yours,
      Mine owne I would say : but [of] mine then yours,
      And so all yours ; O these naughtie times
      Puts bars betweene the owners and their rights .

3   And so though yours, not yours (prove it so)
      Let Fortune goe to hell for it, not I .

4   I speake too long, but 'tis to peize the time,
      To [ich] it, and to draw it out in length,
      To stay you from election .

- amazingly, yet not surprisingly given the circumstances, there are only three capital letters in the whole speech, hardly a sign of mind over matter

- the fact that the F #1 is split into three by the modern texts, and F #2 into four again suggests that, compared to her modern counterpart, Portia's feelings are running away with her verbally as well as emotionally

- this is even more so in the onrushed F #2 which suggests her decision to still abide by her father's will, for she never will be 'forsworne' spills out of her: most modern texts split the decision into three sentences, implying far more rationality than the original Portia seems to be capable of at such a time

- the Freudian slip, in part emotionally formed (by the semicolon) surround phrase ' : but [if] mine then yours/And so all yours ; ' is a complete give away

- and yet there are attempts at self control, with the above phrase and at least three unembellished others, all of which are very important to her desires,

    "I pray you tarrie, pause a day or two/Before you hazard, for in choosing wrong"

    "But least you should not understand me well,/And yet a maiden hath no tongue, but thought,"

    "but 'tis to peize the time,/To [ich] it, and to draw it out in length,/To stay you from election"

which, containing neither long-spelling nor capitals, suggest a tremendous vulnerability, and therefore at these moments she is speaking unadorned, straight from the heart—something very important in an essentially emotional speech (3/20)

The Merchant of Venice

Portia

Away then, I am lockt in one of them,
3.2.40–62

Background: despite wanting to stay with her, Bassanio claims he is on the 'racke', and must to his 'fortune and the caskets'. The following is Portia's response.

Style: initially one on one, in front of a small group, and then to other members of the group

Where: near or in the casket-room

To Whom: Bassanio, with the larger group including Gratiano and Nerrissa, some of Portia's household, and musicians

# of Lines: 23

Probable Timing: 1.10 minutes

Take note: F's five sentences suggest that Portia is much more immediate in connecting and releasing her innermost thoughts than her ten sentence modern equivalent. F's speech falls into two parts, an emotional opening (3/10 the thirteen and a half lines, F #1-4) and a forced control finish (6/4 in the nine and a half onrushed lines of F #5).

Portia

1 Away then !

2   I am lock'd in one of them ;
If you do love me, you will find me out .

3 Nerrissa and the rest, stand all aloof.

4 Let music sound while he doth make his choice ;
Then if he lose he makes a swanlike end,
Fading in music .

5   That the comparison
May stand more proper, my eye shall be the stream
And war'ry death-bed for him .

6   He may win,
And what is music [then] ?

7   [Then] music is
Even as the flourish, when true subjects bow
To a new crowned monarch ; such it is,
As are those dulcet sounds in break of day,
That creep into the dreaming bridegroom's ear,
And summon him to marriage .

8   Now he goes
With no less presence, but with much more love,
Then young Alcides, when he did redeem
The virgin tribute paid by howling Troy
To the sea-monster .

9   I stand for sacrifice ;
The rest aloof are the Dardanian wives,
With bleared visages, come forth to view
The issue of th'exploit .

10   Go, Hercules,
Live thou, I live ; with much much, more dismay
I view the fight [than] thou that mak'st the fray .

Portia

1   Away then, I am lockt in one of them,
    If you doe love me, you will finde me out .

2   Nerryssa and the rest, stand all aloofe,
    Let musicke sound while he doth make his choise,
    Then if he loose he makes a Swan-like end,
    Fading in musique .

3   That the comparison
    May stand more proper, my eye shall be the streame
    And watrie death-bed for him : he may win,
    And what is musique [than] ?

4   [Than] musique is
    Even as the flourish, when true subjects bowe
    To a new crowned Monarch : Such it is,
    As are those dulcet sounds in breake of day,
    That creepe into the dreaming bride-groomes eare,
    And summon him to marriage .

5   Now he goes
    With no lesse presence, but with much more love
    Then yong Alcides, when he did redeeme
    The virgine tribute, paied by howling Troy
    To the Sea-monster : I stand for sacrifice,
    The rest aloofe are the Dardanian wives :
    With bleared visages come forth to view
    The issue of th'exploit : Goe Hercules,
    Live thou, I live with [ ] much more dismay
    I view the fight, [then] thou that mak'st the fray .

- unlike her earlier speech, here Portia is eventually able to bring her somewhat unruly thoughts under control, for though the final F sentence starts from the passion of equal capitals and spellings as she watches Bassanio approach the caskets (3/3 up to the first colon); then, with more capitals than spellings (3/1), she shows her ability to use her considerable mental discipline to draw strength from comparing herself to Dido, the classical heroine of Greece (up to the third colon)—though this doesn't come without a struggle, for the comparison is expressed via two surround phrases; but this seems to work, for after 'Goe Hercules the last two lines are free of any embellishment, as if she is finally under control, no matter how vulnerable

- that this final struggle doesn't come easily is undermined by most modern texts, which split the onrushed F #5 into three

- similarly, F sentences #1-2 move quickly as she begins to face the possibility she may lose Bassanio, a speed most modern texts reduce by splitting each of these F sentences into two

- that she is not under such complete control at the top of the speech as the modern texts suggest is beautifully illustrated by the four tiny F commas at the middle and end of F #1 line one and at the end of the first two lines of F #2, which link somewhat distinct thoughts together far more quickly than the relentlessly logical heavier punctuation (an exclamation mark, a period, and two semicolons) that the modern texts set

- F's longer spelled words emphasize action throughout ('doe love', 'finde', 'loose', 'bowe' 'creepe', 'redeeme', 'Goe'), while, amongst other emotional releases, there is a fixed need for 'musique 3/musicke', as well as the wonderfully hopeful 'bride-groomes eare'

- F #3's surround phrase ' : he may win,/And what is musique then ? ' seems to anticipate her later F #4 'bride-groome' hope , while F #5's surround phrases highlights her understanding of her desperate situation

  " : I stand for sacrifice, /The rest aloofe are the Dardanian wives :/
      With bleared visages come forth to view/The issue of th'exploit : "

Much Adoe About Nothing

Beatrice

Lord, I could not endure a husband with a beard
between 2.1.29- 65

Background: the family are gossiping prior to the Masque to cele-brate Don Pedro's arrival. Beatrice now aims her wit at the idea of husbands, triggered in part by the teasing of both uncles, Leonato and Anthonio, that she will never 'get thee a husband, if thou be so shrewd of thy tongue.'

Style: teasing address to a group of intimates

Where: at the house of her uncle Leonato wherever the Masque is about to begin (indoors or outdoors is unspecified)

To Whom: Leonato, Hero, her uncle Anthonio with perhaps others of the household

# of Lines: 21

Probable Timing: 1.10 minutes

Take note: save for the opening phrase there are very few phrases where Beatrice does not show some form of vocal release (mainly emotional, 11/27 overall)—it seems the party has got to her a little, anticipation of the forthcoming festivities perhaps (even a drink or two) has begun to loosen her tongue.

Beatrice

1   Lord, I could not endure a husband with a
beard on his face, I had rather lie in the woollen !

2   {As for}a husband that hath
no beard ? {w}hat should I do with him ? dress him in
my apparel and make him my waiting gentlewoman ?

3   He
that hath a beard is more [than] a youth, and he that hath
no beard is less [than] a man ; and he that is more [than] a
youth is not for me, and he that is less [than] a man, I am
not for him ; therefore I will even take sixpence in earnest
of the [bear-ward], and lead his apes {to the gates of} hell .

---

4   And there will the devil
meet me like an old cuckold with horns on his head,
and say, "Get you to heaven, Beatrice, get you to heaven,
here's no place for you maids."

5   So deliver I up my apes,
and way to [Saint] Peter .

6   For the heavens, he shows me
where the bachelors sit, and there live we as merry as
the day is long .

---

7 {†}   {I will never be} fitted with a husband
  {†} till God make men of some other metal [than] earth .

8   Would it not grieve a woman to be overmaster'd
with a piece of valiant dust ? to make [an] account of
her life to a clod of wayward marl ?

9   No, uncle, I'll none .

10   Adam's sons are my brethren, and truly I hold it a sin
to match in my kinred .

Beatrice

1   Lord, I could not endure a husband with a
beard on his face, I had rather lie in the woollen .

2   {As for}a husband that hath
no beard ? {w}hat should I doe with him ? dresse him in
my apparell, and make him my waiting gentlewoman ? he
that hath a beard, is more [then] a youth : and he that hath
no beard, is lesse [then] a man : and hee that is more [then] a
youth, is not for mee : and he that is lesse [then] a man, I am
not for him : therefore I will even take sixepence in earnest
of the [Berrord], and leade his Apes {to the gates of} hell .

---

3   And there will the Devill
meete mee like an old Cuckold with hornes on his head,
and say, get you to heaven Beatrice, get you to heaven,
heere's no place for you maids, so deliver I up my Apes,
and way to [S.] Peter : for the heavens, hee shewes mee
where the Batchellers sit, and there live wee as merry as
the day is long .

---

4 {†} {I will never be} fitted with a husband
  {†} till God make men of some other mettall [then] earth,
would it not grieve a woman to be over-mastred
with a peece of valiant dust ? to make [ ] account of
her life to a clod of waiward marle ? no unckle, ile none :
Adams sonnes are my brethren, and truly I hold it a sinne
to match in my kinred .

- after the almost thesis like quality of the shortish opening sentence (0/1), the onrushed F 2-4 show what a fine roll she is on, highlighting her ability to spin out a complex, seemingly never-ending, stream of thoughts building one on top of another (most modern texts make her work much harder, and therefore her wit a little heavier, by turning F's three sentences into nine)

- the superb relentlessness of F #2, dismissing both mature and young men alike, is underscored by all seven and half lines being completely formed by eight surround phrases—the hardest working sentence of the speech, and the fun of this is obviously emotional (2/9)

- allowing herself to relish the thoughts of abandoning all her man-'Apes' in hell leads to the only intellectual release in the speech and even this is almost matched by emotional delight (6/4, the first four lines of F #3), while her dreams of being 'merry as the day is long' with the 'Batchellers' in heaven becomes emotional once more (1/5, the last two lines of F #3)

- interestingly, in the finale, though her refusal to be fitted with a husband seems to start out in full and easy control (1/1 in the first three lines of F #4, to the first question-mark), the refusal becomes much more emotional by the finish (1/5 in the last three lines), no matter how witty the images may seem to be

Much Adoe About Nothing

Hero

Good Margaret runne thee to the parlour,
between 3.1.1–33

Background: and now the women begin their part of the plot. As such, each speech is self-explanatory, this speech sets up how they are going to do it.

Style: a three-handed scene

Where: the gardens at Leonato's

To Whom: to Margaret in front of Ursula, and then to to Ursula;

# of Lines: 26

Probable Timing: 1.15 minutes

Take Note: Though the last two sentences almost match, the onrush of F # 1 and #2 suggest much more excitement for Hero as the speech opens (as befits a young woman about to trick her cousin into re-falling in love) than the modern texts which, by splitting F #1 into five and F #2 into four, create a series of much more rational instructions and comments.

Hero

1   Good Margaret, run thee to the parlor,
      There shalt thou find my Cousin Beatrice
      Proposing with the Prince and Claudio .

2   Whisper her ear, and tell her I and Ursula,
      Walk in the orchard, and our whole discourse
      Is all of her .

3   Say that thou overheardst us,
      And bid her steal into the pleached bower,
      Where honeysuckles ripened by the sun,
      Forbid the sun to enter, like favorites,
      Made proud by princes, that advance their pride
      Against that power that bred it .

4   There will she hide her,
      To listen our [propose] .

5   This is thy office ;
      Bear thee well in it, and leave us alone .

---

6   Now, Ursula, when Beatrice doth come,
      As we do trace this alley up and down,
      Our talk must only be of Benedick .

7   When I do name him, let it be thy part
      To praise him more [than] ever man did merit .

8   My talk to thee must be how Benedick
      Is sick in love with Beatrice .

9   Of this matter
      Is little Cupids crafty arrow made,
      That only wounds by hearsay .

10   Now begin,
      For look where Beatrice like a lapwing runs
      Close by the ground, to hear our conference .

---

11   Then go we near her, that her ear lose nothing
      Of the false sweet bait that we lay for it {.}

Hero

1   Good Margaret runne thee to the parlour,
There shalt thou finde my Cosin Beatrice,
Proposing with the Prince and Claudio,
Whisper her eare, and tell her I and Ursula,
Walke in the Orchard, and our whole discourse
Is all of her, say that thou over-heardst us,
And bid her steale into the pleached bower,
Where hony-suckles ripened by the sunne,
Forbid the sunne to enter : like favourites,
Made proud by Princes, that advance their pride,
Against that power that bred it, there will she hide her,
To listen our [purpose], this is thy office,
Beare thee well in it, and leave us alone .

---

2   Now Ursula, when Beatrice doth come,
As we do trace this alley up and downe,
Our talke must onely be of Benedicke,
When I doe name him, let it be thy part,
To praise him more [then] ever man did merit,
My talke to thee must be how Benedicke
Is sicke in love with Beatrice : of this matter,
Is little Cupids crafty arrow made,
That onely wounds by heare-say : now begin,
For looke where Beatrice like a Lapwing runs
Close by the ground, to heare our conference .

---

3   Then go we neare her that her eare loose nothing,
Of the false sweete baite that we lay for it :

- while setting up the factual details of the scam for Margaret to follow may of necessity be intellectual, there still seems a fair amount of
emotion involved (7/8, F #1's first eight and a half lines to the only
colon in the sentence)—anticipation perhaps?, especially since the
capitals disappear after the first five lines

- following the colon, a much more careful and calm elaboration is
offered as to how Beatrice will behave ('there will she hide her,/To
listen our purpose', 1/2, the last four and half lines)

- that Margaret and Ursula are not yet ready to move (finding this
elaboration perhaps enjoyable or even somewhat startling) might be
seen in the ungrammatical fast-link comma by which Hero moves
on into the sentence—ending instruction 'this is thy office', which
starts halfway through the penultimate line: most modern texts remove this possibility by setting the instruction as a separate sentence
(mt. #5)

- the instructions to Ursula are equally intellectual with even more
emotional involvement (8/12, F #2)

- and then excited determination takes over, both as to how she in-
tends to operate (the first colon), and the instruction to let the tempt-
ing start (the second)

  " : of this matter,/Is little Cupids crafty arrow made,/That onely
    wounds

by heare-say : now begin . "

- that 'now begin' continues F's sentence (#2) rather, than as most
modern texts set it, starting a new one (mt. #10) suggests that Hero is
more excited than her modern text counterpart

- and the excitement seems to be emotional, for after the passion of
spotting where and how Beatrice is trying to hide, the (exciting?) suggestion that they go near her is totally non-intellectual (0/5, F #3)

The Merry Wives of Windsor

Mistris Page

{Did you ever heare the like ? }
2.1.68–93

Background: joined by her closest friend, Mistris Ford, Mistris Page discovers to her amazement, and presumably growing righteous anger, that Falstaffe has sent them exactly the same letters, despite the fact that both are married. One note: the opening sentence, marked {†}, was originally assigned to Mistris Ford.

Style: as part of a two-handed scene

Where: unspecified, presumably a public place in the town of Windsor

To Whom: Mistris Ford

# of Lines: 19

Probable Timing: 1.00 minutes

Take note: The speech starts as confusedly as the previous one ended, with its onrushed start finally settling down into a slightly more composed finish.

Mistris Page

1 {†}   {Did you ever
hear the like ? }

2   Letter for letter ; but that the name of
Page and Ford differs!

3   To thy great comfort in this my-
stery of ill opinions, here's the twin-brother of thy letter ; but let thine inherit first, for I protest mine never
shall .

4   I warrant he hath a thousand of these letters, writ
with blank space for different names (sure, more!) ;and
these are of the second edition .

5   He will print them, out
of doubt ;for he cares not what he puts into the press,
when he would put us two .

6   I had rather be a giantess,
and lie under Mount Pelion .

7   Well—I will find you twenty lascivious turtles ere one chaste man .{†}

8   What doth
he think of us ? {†}

9   It makes me almost ready to wrangle with mine own honesty .

10   I'll entertain
myself like one that I am not acquainted withal; for
sure unless he know some strain in me that I know
not myself, he would never have boarded me in this
fury .

11   "Boarding," call {I} it ?

12   I'll be sure to keep
him above deck .

13 {†}   If he come under my hatches,
I'll never to sea again .

Mistris Page

1 {†}   {Did you ever
heare the like ? }

2   Letter for letter ;but that the name of
Page and Ford differs :to thy great comfort in this my-
stery of ill opinions, heere's the twyn-brother of thy Letter : but let thine inherit first, for I protest mine never
shall :I warrant he hath a thousand of these Letters, writ
with blancke-space for different names (sure more) : and
these are of the second edition :hee will print them out
of doubt : for he cares not what hee puts into the presse,
when he would put us two :I had rather be a Giantesse,
and lye under Mount Pelion :Well ; I will find you twen-
tie lascivious Turtles ere one chaste man .{†}

3   What doth
he thinke of us ? {†}

4   It makes me almost rea-
die to wrangle with mine owne honesty :Ile entertaine
my selfe like one that I am not acquainted withall : for
sure unlesse hee know some straine in mee, that I know
not my selfe, hee would never have boorded me in this
furie .

5   Boording, call {I} it ?

6   Ile bee sure to keepe
him above decke .

7 {†}   If hee come under my hatches,
Ile never to Sea againe .

- she opens with a (startled?) very short sentence (0/1, F #1), while the onrushed F #2 shows no consistency whatsoever, as both the switches in style and the surround phrases clearly show

- F #2's emotionally (semicolon) created surround phrases underscore Mistris Page's rightful indignation

  " . Letter for letter ; but that the name of Page and Ford differs : "

  " : Well ; I will find you twenty lascivious Turtles ere one chaste man . "

  while the more controlled (colon) surround phrases of F #2 add extra weight to her self-deprecating ridicule of Falstaffe

 " : and these are of the second edition: hee will print them out of doubt : for he cares not what hee puts into the presse, when he would put us two : I had rather be a Giantesse, and lye under Mount Pelion : "

- in terms of style, while she starts out F #2 intellectually (2/0, the first surround-phrases line), she then becomes passionate in both denying any interest in taking the invitation up, and in beginning to comprehend his 'thousand of these Letters' method of operation (2/3, the next four and a half lines); this in turn becomes emotional as she elaborates even more on 'the second edition' nature of his wooing (0/3 the next two and a half lines), but she finishes more intellectually than emotionally with a two line absolute refusal ('I had rather...lye under Mount Pelion') and sentence ending surround phrase maxim (4/2)

- but this momentary intellectual control does not last, for the rest of the speech becomes almost totally emotional (1/17 in the remaining nine lines comprising F #3-7)

- whether this final emotion is all high powered indignation or eventually turns into something more light hearted is up to each actress to decide, though the shortness of the last three sentences (F #5-7) are certainly different in content from the onrushed F #4, the speech ending with a much earthier sense of humour directed towards herself

As You Like It
Celia

{†} **I see thou lov'st mee not with the full**
between 1.2.8–23

Background:, Celia's father, the new Duke, Fredericke, did not include Rosalind in the recent banishment of her father, Duke Senior, only because he knows that Celia and Rosalind, 'being ever from their Cradles bred together', are, in Celia's own words, inseparable as 'Juno's Swans'. Nevertheless, Celia is fearful for Rosalind's well-being: hence the following.

Style: as part of a two-handed scene

Where: unspecified, but presumably somewhere inside or outside the palace where the two cousins meet to be alone

To Whom: her cousin Rosalind

# of Lines: 12

Probable Timing: 0.40 minutes

Take note: With four semicolons in this twelve-line speech, it seems that Celia is in more than just a teasing mood.

Celia

1 {†}   I see thou lov'st me not with the full
weight that I love thee .

2   If my uncle, thy banished father,
had banished thy uncle, the Duke my father, so thou
hadst been still with me, I could have taught my love
to take thy father for mine ; so wouldst thou, if the truth
of thy love to me were so righteously temper'd as mine
is to thee .

---

3   You know my father hath no child but I, nor
none is like to have ; and truly when he dies, thou shalt
be his heir; for what he hath taken away from thy father perforce, I will render thee again in affection .

4   By
mine honour, I will, and when I break that oath, let me
turn monster .

5   Therefore, my sweet Rose, my dear Rose,
be merry .

Celia

1 {†}   I see thou lov'st mee not with the full
waight that I love thee ; if my Uncle thy banished father
had banished thy Uncle the Duke my Father, so thou
hadst beene still with mee, I could have taught my love
to take thy father for mine ; so wouldst thou, if the truth
of thy love to me were so righteously temper'd, as mine
is to thee .

---

2   You know my Father hath no childe, but I, nor
none is like to have ; and truely when he dies, thou shalt
be his heire ; for what hee hath taken away from thy father perforce, I will render thee againe in affection : by
mine honor I will, and when I breake that oath, let mee
turne monster : therefore my sweet Rose, my deare Rose,
be merry .

- the fact that one or other of them (or both) may be in a fragile state might be seen in the serious extended unembellished passage that closes F #1. viz.

  "I could have taught my love to take thy father for mine ; so wouldst thou, if the truth of thy love to me were so righteously temper'd, as mine is to thee ."

- the speech opens passionately (4/3 the first three lines of F #1), and continues with the unembellished ending of F #1, but it seems Celia cannot maintain self-control any further, for in offering to disinherit herself the speech becomes highly emotional (1/8), though she does manage to close intellectually as she begs her cousin to 'be merry' (2/1 the last line of F #2)

- the emotional surround phrases underscore her love for her cousin

  " . I see thou lov'st mee not with the full waight that I love thee ; "

  " ; so wouldst thou, if the truth of thy love to me were so righteous-ly temper'd, as mine is to thee . "

  to the extent of disinheriting herself as a future ruler of the Dukedom

  " . You know my Father hath no childe, but I, nor none is like to have ; and truely when he dies, thou shalt be his heire ; "

  while the final logical (colon created) surround phrases stress the in-tegrity of her promise, as well as her love once more

  " : by mine honor I will, and when I breake that oath, let mee turne monster : therefore my sweet Rose, my deare Rose, be merry ."

As You Like It

Rosalind

Love is meerely a madnesse, and I tel you,...
between 3.2.400–427

Background: accidentally meeting Orlando in the woods, Rosalind embarks on the biggest bluff in her life in an attempt to see him more often

Style: both, as part of a three-handed scene

Where: somewhere in the woods

To Whom: both, Orlando in front of Celia

# of Lines: 23

Probable Timing: 1.10 minutes

Take note: Interestingly, F's onrushed F #4 and its orthography suggests that the idea of how Rosalind will deal with Orlando grows slowly, for it starts unembellished but ends full of passionate release—yet she might not be as confident as the words would suggest, for there are nearly twenty short spellings.

Rosalind

1   Love is merely a madness, and I tell you, de-
serves as well a dark house and a whip as madmen do ;
and the reason why they are not so punish'd and cured is,
that the lunacy is so ordinary that the whippers are in
love too .

2   Yet I profess curing it by counsel .

3   {I cured one,} and in this manner .

4   He was to ima-
gine me his love, his mistress ; and I set him every day
to woo me .

5   At which time would I, being but a moonish
youth, grieve, be effeminate, changeable, longing and
liking, proud, fantastical, apish, shallow, inconstant, full
of tears, full of smiles ; for every passion something, and
for no passion truly any thing, as boys and women are
for the most part, cattle of this color ; would now like
him, now loathe him ; then entertain him, then forswear
him ; now weep for him, then spit at him ; that I drave
my suitor from his mad humor of love to a living humor
of madness, [which] was, to forswear the full stream of
[the] world, and to live in a nook merely monastic .

6   And thus I cur'd
him, and this way will I take upon me to wash your liver as clean as a sound sheep's heart, that there shall not
be one spot of love in't .

7   I would cure you, if you would but call me Rosalind, and come every day to my cote and woo me .

Rosalind

1   Love is meerely a madnesse, and I tel you, de-
serves as wel a darke house, and a whip, as madmen do :
and the reason why they are not so punish'd and cured, is
that the Lunacie is so ordinarie, that the whippers are in
love too : yet I professe curing it by counsel .

2   {I cured one,} and in this manner .

3   Hee was to imagine me his Love, his Mistris : and I set him everie day
to woe me .

4   At which time would I, being but a moonish
youth, greeve, be effeminate, changeable, longing, and
liking, proud, fantastical, apish, shallow, inconstant, ful
of teares, full of smiles ; for everie passion something, and
for no passion truly any thing, as boyes and women are
for the most part, cattle of this colour : would now like
him, now loath him : then entertaine him, then forswear
him : now weepe for him, then spit at him ; that I drave
my Sutor from his mad humor of love, to a living humor
of madnes, [w] was to forsweare the ful stream of [ÿ] world,
and to live in a nooke meerly Monastick : and thus I cur'd
him, and this way wil I take upon mee to wash your Liver as cleane as a sound sheepes heart, that there shal not
be one spot of Love in't .

5   I would cure you, if you would but call me Rosalind, and come everie day to my Coat, and woe me .

- since the speech represents one of the most important actions in Rosalind's life, for if she succeeds she can see so much more of Orlando without revealing herself, it's not surprising that the opening (F #1-3) is triply highlighted

  a. by the four extra breath-thoughts (marked ,), adding extra details as to how/why lovers are not 'punish'd and cured'

  b. the surround phrases emphasising how she has supposedly cured one other person in love, ' : yet I professe curing it by counsel . ', and the whole F #3, ' . Hee was to imagine me his Love, his Mistris : and I set him everie day to woe me .', the first highly released (2/1) and the second overly controlled with short spellings of 'everie' and 'woe'

  c. emphasised by the unembellished short sentence F #2, 'I cured one, and in this manner.'

- in the onrushed F #4, the emotional semicolons mark off three distinct stages of development/release

  a. the opening three lines, describing in general how she behaved (supposedly) as the ever changeable 'moonish youth' are unembellished with the exception of the one word 'teares'

  b. the next four lines (incorporating at least three surround phrases) describing the tremendous opposites she (supposedly) inflicted upon the (supposed) victim, start becoming emotional (0/4)

  c. and then the final summation, of how her 'Sutor' supposedly went to 'live in a nooke meerly Monastick' and how she can do the same for Orlando, is offered via a pronounced and extended flourish (4/7 in the final six lines of F #4)

- and, again understandable given the enormity of the decision he is about to make in accepting or rejecting her offer, so her final 'I would cure you' is a wondrous mixture of controlled intellect (2/0, F #5), unembellished phrases, and a single extra-breath—the combination underlying and undermining her apparent outward calm

As You Like It

Phebe

I would not be thy executioner,
between 3.58–34

Background: until meeting the disguised Rosalind Phebe seems to have a healthy scepticisim whenever love is expressed in exaggerated hyperbole. Here is her factual response to Silvius' plea not to be sterner than an executioner.

Style: as part of a two-handed scene

Where: somewhere in the woods, near the cottage of Rosalind and Celia

To Whom: Silvius

# of Lines: 23

Probable Timing: 1.10 minutes

Take note: It seems that most of the time Phebe can answer Silvius with relative ease, for though, in comparison to most modern texts, F's first two sentences are onrushed (F #1 usually being split into two, and F #2 in three), the dismissal of each of his points is handled by a very logical colon, with little or no extra release, save for a couple of ridiculing moments.

Phebe

1   I would not be thy executioner ;
     I fly thee for I would not injure thee .

2   Thou tell'st me there is murder in mine eye :
     'Tis pretty, sure, and very probable,
     That eyes, that are the frail'st and softest things,
     Who shut their coward gates on atomies,
     Should be called tyrants, butchers, murtherers!

3   Now I do frown on thee with all my heart,
     And if mine eyes can wound, now let them kill thee .

4   Now counterfeit to swound ; why, now fall down,
     Or if thou canst not, O, for shame, for shame,
     Lie not, to say mine eyes are murtherers !

5   Now show the wound mine eye hath made in thee,
     Scratch thee but with a pin, and there remains
     Some scar of it ; lean [but] upon a rush,
     The cicatrice and capable impressure
     Thy palm some moment keeps ; but now mine eyes,
     Which I have darted at thee, hurt thee not,
     Nor I am sure there is no force in eyes
     That can doe[any] hurt .

---

6   Come not thou near me ; and {if} that time {should come},
     Afflict me with thy mocks, pity me not,
     As till that time I shall not pity thee .

Phebe

1 I would not be thy executioner,
   I flye thee, for I would not injure thee :
   Thou tellst me there is murder in mine eye
   'Tis pretty sure, and very probable,
   That eyes that are the frailst, and softest things,
   Who shut their coward gates on atomyes,
   Should be called tyrants, butchers, murtherers .

2 Now I doe frowne on thee with all my heart,
   And if mine eyes can wound, now let them kill thee :
   Now counterfeit to swound, why now fall downe,
   Or if thou canst not, oh for shame, for shame,
   Lye not, to say mine eyes are murtherers :
   Now shew the wound mine eye hath made in thee,
   Scratch thee but with a pin, and there remaines
   Some scarre of it : Leane [ ] upon a rush
   The Cicatrice and capable impressure
   Thy palme some moment keepes : but now mine eyes
   Which I have darted at thee, hurt thee not,
   Nor I am sure there is no force in eyes
   That can doe [ ]hurt .

---

3 Come not thou neere me : and {if} that time {should come},
   Afflict me with thy mockes, pitty me not,
   As till that time I shall not pitty thee .

- thus, in her opening denial of being his 'executioner' and that eyes should be called 'tyrants, butchers, murtherers', she hardly breaks into a sweat (0/2 in the seven lines of F #1)

- mocking his idea of her being able to kill him because 'Now I doe frowne' releases some momentary emotion (0/2 the first line of F #2), and then she relaxes into a calm unembellished second line: calling him out as a liar if he cannot be so killed raises a little emotion once more (0/3 in the next four lines), though whether the emotions are amusement or annoyance is up to each actress to explore

- and then, as she demands to see 'the wound mine eye hath made in thee' since even the tiniest of things (a pin scratch or leaning on a rush will leave a 'scarre' or some 'impressure'), the releases become slightly more marked (2/5 in the next four and a half lines)

- but this momentary outburst subsides in the final all but unembellished three lines that end F #2, with only the final 'doe' in 'doe hurt' showing any release

- but, by her final monosyllabic surround phrase command ' . Come not thou neere me : ' and ensuing invitation for 'mockes', it seems as if something has given way, for in comparison to what has gone on before the whole sentence is quite emotional (0/4 in F #3's three lines)

As You Like It

Rosalind

No faith, die by Attorney : the poore world
4.1.94–108

Background: having succeeded via the previous speech in persuading
Orlando to come to the cottage where she and Celia dwell so that
she could wash his 'Liver as cleane as a sound sheepes heart' and
thus cure him of his love, she now lets loose with several quasi cyn-
ical statements as to love, though it's useful to remember that as
far as she is concerned she has been abandoned twice by men who
purported to love her—her father and her uncle.

Style: both, as part of a three-handed scene

Where: somewhere in the woods near to her cottage

To Whom: both, Orlando in front of Celia

# of Lines: 13

Probable Timing: 0.45 minutes

Take note: Fascinatingly, F suggests that here Rosalind goes directly
against the conventional notion that a speech should start small
and end big.

Rosalind

1   No, faith, die by attorney .

2   The poor world is
almost six thousand years old, and in all this time there
was not any man died in his own person, videlicet, in
a love-cause .

3   Troilus had his brains dash'd out with a
Grecian club, yet he did what he could to die before,
and he is one of the patterns of love .

4   Leander, he would
have liv'd many a fair year though Hero had turn'd
nun, if it had not been for a hot midsummer night ;
for, good youth, he went but forth to wash him in the Hel-
lespont, and being taken with the cramp was drown'd;
and the foolish chroniclers of that age found it was -
Hero of [Sestos] .

5   But these are all lies : men have died
from time to time, and worms have eaten them, but not
for love .

Rosalind

1   No faith, die by Attorney : the poore world is
almost six thousand yeeres old, and in all this time there
was not anie man died in his owne person (videlicet) in
a love cause : Troilous had his braines dash'd out with a
Grecian club, yet he did what hee could to die before,
and he is one of the patternes of love .

2   Leander, he would
have liv'd manie a faire yeere though Hero had turn'd
Nun ; if it had not bin for a hot Midsomer-night, for
(good youth) he went but forth to wash him in the Hel-
lespont, and being taken with the crampe, was droun'd,
and the foolish Chronoclers of that age, found it was
Hero of [Cestos] .

3   But these are all lies, men have died
from time to time, and wormes have eaten them, but not
for love .

- with Rosalind's opening denial of any male dying for love (not even the traditional epitome 'Troilous'), the speech starts out powerfully (via the opening surround phrase) and emotionally (3/7 in F #1's five and a half lines)

- and then dismissing Leander, the other icon of supposed male fidelity, the speech becomes highly intellectual (8/4 in six and a half lines of F #2), though the dismissal of the accident of a 'hot Midsomer-night' is heralded by the only (emotional) semicolon in the speech, and the finish of the sentence is accompanied by two F only extra breath-thoughts(marked ,)—as if she need the extra breaths to control her intellectual anger/defiance/scorn/amusement

- and then all energy seems leached out of her for the final summation of 'these are all lies', for Rosalind's final sentence is very quiet in comparison with what has gone on before (0/1, F #3)

Twelfe Night, or, what you will

Viola

There is a faire behaviour in thee Captaine,
between 1.2.46–64

Background: Viola, travelling with her beloved twin-brother Sebastian, has been ship-wrecked, and believes (incorrectly as it turns out) that she alone was saved, and he drowned. Having lost everything in the wreck, having no means to provide for herself, and learning that the gentle and generous sea-captain has brought her to Illyria, whose Duke (Orsino) her deceased father knew and spoke well of, Viola decides to disguise herself as a neutered male (a eunuch) and enter his service.

Style: one on one perhaps in front of a small group

Where: on the sea-shore of Illyria

Whom: the Sea-Captaine perhaps in front of a small group of sailors

# of Lines: 16

Probable Timing: 0.50 minutes

Take Note: The enormity of what she is about to propose, and the personal risk she is taking, can be seen in the excessive releases of the first line of the speech (1/3): from then on the remaining (mainly emotional, 3/11) releases all enhance the idea she is exploring and/or the argument she is presenting.

Viola

1   There is a fair behavior in thee, captain,
     And though that nature with a beauteous wall
     Doth oft close in pollution, yet of thee
     I [well] believe thou hast a mind that suits
     With this thy fair and outward character .

2   I prithee (and I'll pay thee bounteously)
     Conceal me what I am, and be my aid
     For such disguise as haply shall become
     The form of my intent .

3   I'll serve this duke ;
     Thou shalt present me as an eunuch to him,
     It may be worth thy pains ; for I can sing
     And speak to him in many sorts of music
     That will allow me very worth his service .

4   What else may hap, to time I will commit,
     Only shape thou thy silence to my wit .

---

5 {†} Lead me on .

Viola

1   There is a faire behaviour in thee Captaine,
     And though that nature, with a beauteous wall
     Doth oft close in pollution : yet of thee
     I [will] beleeve thou hast a minde that suites
     With this thy faire and outward charracter .

2   I prethee (and Ile pay thee bounteously)
     Conceale me what I am, and be my ayde,
     For such disguise as haply shall become
     The forme of my intent .

3   Ile serve this Duke,
     Thou shalt present me as an Eunuch to him,
     It may be worth thy paines : for I can sing,
     And speake to him in many sorts of Musicke,
     That will allow me very worth his service .

4   What else may hap, to time I will commit,
     Onely shape thou thy silence to my wit

---

5 {†} Lead me on .

- sometimes these come in clusters, as with her initially unembellished first thoughts (the first phrase of F #1) and her decision to trust the Captaine (0/5 the last two lines of F #1)

    "I will beleeve thou hast a minde that suites/With this thy faire and outward charracter ."

- but mostly they come as a single key word in each phrase, as she uses the term 'prethee' to the Captaine, to 'ayde' her to 'conceale' her identity, and later explains she will 'speake' to the Duke via many forms of 'Musicke'

- the one moment of intellect in the speech comes as she realises that there may be a way out of her current dilemma, 'Ile serve this Duke' by disguising herself as an 'Eunuch' and make her way in his service by her ability in 'Musicke'

- given the enormity of the decisions within the speech, the very short unembellished monosyllabic final sentence 'Lead me on.', while often played as a triumphant conclusion, suggests rather that Viola may be attempting to enforce an appearance of calm which she may not necessarily be feeling

Twelfe Night, or, what you will

Olivia

What is your Parentage ?
between 1.5.289–311

Background: Viola's naked passion, spurred no doubt by her unspoken love for Orsino, proves too much for Olivia, who, quite obviously, is mightily smitten by the attractive 'boy' (Viola as Cesario) to the point of falling in love. When the opening question was originally asked, the answer was all-important, for if Cesario/Viola was of anything other than 'gentle' birth, Olivia could hold no hopes of any possible relationship, the social gap between them would have been far too big. However, Viola's response 'I am a Gentleman' was exactly what Olivia wanted to hear.

Style: solo

Where: somewhere in Olivia's palace

To Whom: self, and direct audience address

# of Lines: 15

Probable Timing: 0.50 minutes

Take note: The speech is a wonderful mi of short bursts of intellect, unembellished lines, and emotion—a sure sign that, for now, Olivia cannot keep herself in check.

Olivia

1   "What is your parentage ? "

2   "Above my fortunes, yet my state is well :
    I am a gentleman ."

3   I'll be sworn thou art ;
    Thy tongue, thy face, thy limbs, actions, and spirit,
    Do give thee five fold blazon .

4   Not too fast ! soft, soft!

5   Unless the master were the man .

6   How now ?

7   Even so quickly may one catch the plague ?

8   [Methinks] I feel this youth's perfections
    With an invisible, and subtle stealth
    To creep in at mine eyes .

9   Well, let it be .

10 What ho, Malvolio !

---

11 I do I know not what, and fear to find
    Mine eye too great a flatterer for my mind.

12 Fate, show thy force : our selves we do not owe ;
    What is decreed, must be ; and be this so .

Olivia

1   What is your Parentage ?

2   Above my fortunes, yet my state is well ;
    I am a Gentleman .

3   Ile be sworne thou art,
    Thy tongue, thy face, thy limbes, actions, and spirit,
    Do give thee five-fold blazon : not too fast: soft, soft,
    Unlesse the Master were the man .

4   How now ?

5   Even so quickly may one catch the plague ?

6   [Me thinkes] I feele this youths perfections
    With an invisible, and subtle stealth
    To creepe in at mine eyes .

7   Well, let it be .

8   What hoa, Malvolio .

---

9   I do I know not what, and feare to finde
    Mine eye too great a flatterer for my minde :
    Fate, shew thy force, our selves we do not owe,
    What is decreed, must be : and be this so .

- while the speech seems to open in control (2/0 the first two sentences), the fact that F #1 is so short, and F #2 made up of two emotional (thanks to the semicolon) surround phrases, suggests that the control may be difficult to establish, especially since the simple fact of F #2's '. Above my fortunes, yet my state is well ; / I am a Gentleman . ' means Olivia can in all good conscience chase after 'Cesario' since their difference in rank is not all that insurmountable

- dwelling on 'Cesario's' physical attributes, and wishing 'he' were wooing for 'himself' instead of for Orsino, emotions creep in (1/3, F #3) despite her strong admonition of caution to herself, via the unembellished monosyllabic surround phrase ' : not too fast : '

- and the (awful? joyous?) realisation that she has caught the 'plague' of love is also unembellished (F #5), as if the words can scarcely be uttered aloud

- and though Olivia's immediate response to her feeling ('I feele' rather than think) about 'the youths perfections' is emotional once more (0/2, F 6), the decision to 'Well, let it be.' is again very quiet, and triply weighted in being monosyllabic, unembellished, and a short sentence (F #8)

- her commitment to action, (calling in Malvolio via another very short sentence

- (F #8) is passionate, and though her immediate response to having done so is purely emotional (0/3, the first two lines of F #9), her handing herself over to 'Fate' is totally unembellished again, with the short monosyllabic surround-phrase ending the speech ' : and be this so : ' sounding remarkably like a prayer for success

Twelfe Night, or, what you will

Viola

I but I know.
between 2.4.103–218

Background: in a sort of locker-room man-to-man discussion (as Orsino believes) with 'Cesario' as to the differences in intensity between male and female love, Orsino suggests that men, especially he, feel things far more deeply than any woman could, dismissing women's love as mere 'appetite'. The following is Viola's response, and it's up to each actress to decide just how successfully Viola manages to maintain her male pose and poise throughout the speech.

Style: as part of a two-handed scene

Where: somewhere in Orsino's palace

To Whom: her unspoken love, Orsino

# of Lines: 14

Probable Timing: 0.45 minutes

Take note: F's orthography clearly shows that, despite a very determined attempt to control her emotions, as the speech progresses, so Viola's emotions swamp what vestiges of the self-control she opened with.

Viola

1   Ay, but I know—
     Too well what love women to men may owe ;
     In faith, they are as true of heart, as we .

2   My father had a daughter lov'd a man
     As it might be perhaps, were I a woman,
     I should your lordship .

---

3 {†}   She never told her love,
     But let concealment like a worm i'th bud
     Feed on her damask cheek ; she pin'd in thought,
     And with a green and yellow melancholy
     She [sat] like Patience on a monument,
     Smiling at grief .

4   Was not this love indeed ?

5   We men may say more, swear more, but indeed
     Our shows are more [than] will ; for still we prove
     Much in our vows, but little in our love

Viola

1   I but I know.

2   Too well what love women to men may owe :
    In faith they are as true of heart, as we .

3   My Father had a daughter lov'd a man
    As it might be perhaps, were I a woman
    I should your Lordship .

---

4 {†}   She never told her love,
    But let concealment like a worme i'th budde
    Feede on her damaske cheeke : she pin'd in thought,
    And with a greene and yellow melancholly,
    She [sate] like Patience on a Monument,
    Smiling at greefe .

5   Was not this love indeede ?

6   We men may say more, sweare more, but indeed
    Our shewes are more [then] will : for still we prove
    Much in our vowes, but little in our love .

- F's orthography clearly shows that, despite a very determined attempt to control her emotions, as the speech progresses, so Viola's emotions swamp what vestiges of the self-control she opened with.

- that F #1-2 are unembellished; F #2 is made up of two surround phrases; and F #3 is purely factual (2/), are all excellent indicators of her attempts at self-control—while the peculiar opening of a second ungrammatical sentence after the first four words of the speech suggests that she is struggling very hard to maintain the surface demeanor of objectivity

- but following the unembellished statement opening F #3 'She never told her love', as the 'concealment' is touched upon (her own of course, for she is the only daughter her father had), so emotion simply floods in (2/13 in just the eight lines that end the speech)

- the small clues of the very short sentence F #5, 'Was not this love indeede?' and two of the three surround phrases, first the unembellished statement that she knows

  " . Too well what love women to men may owe ; "

and second, in her disguised persona Cesario, how men usually behave

  " : for still we prove/Much in our vowes, but little in our love . "

again point to her love-wounded vulnerability

Twelfe Night, or, what you will
Olivia

y'are servant to the Count Orsino youth .
between 3.1.100–122

Background: despite knowing of Olivia's feelings for her disguised persona as Cesario, Viola has had to return to Olivia, very unwillingly, to pursue Orsino's wooing. Olivia doesn't even know Viola's disguised self's name, and has thus asked the seemingly innocent question 'What is your name'. However, moments before Olivia has actually tried to touch Viola, under the guise of the request 'Give me your hand sir.', which of course, as a supposed servant, Viola/Cesario should never do except in carefully prescribed circumstances (helping on an awkward or dirty pathway for example). Thus, though seemingly answering Olivia's request as to his/her name, Viola takes great care in her reply 'Cesario is your servants name, faire Princesse' to remind Olivia of the servant-mistress gap between them. However, Olivia will have none of it, or of Orsino either.

Where: the gardens of Olivia's home

To Whom: Viola disguised as Cesario

# of Lines: 19

Probable Timing: 1.00 minutes

Take Note: F's orthography shows how and when Olivia fails to maintain self-control, especially when Viola/Cesario refuses to respond to any of her blandishments (and whether Olivia is genuine in her apologies or merely playing femme fatale is up to each actress to explore).

Olivia

1   Y'are servant to the Count Orsino, youth .

---

2   For him, I think not on him .
                              For his thoughts,
     Would they were blanks, rather than fill'd with me .

---

3 {†} I {bid} you never speak again of him ;
     But would you undertake another suit,
     I had rather hear you, to solicit that
     [Than] music from the spheres .

---

4   Give me leave, beseech you .

5   I did send,
     After the last enchantment you did [here],
     A ring in chase of you ;so did I abuse
     Myself, my servant, and I fear me you .

6   Under your hard construction must I sit,
     To force that on you in a shameful cunning
     Which you knew none of yours .

7   What might you think ?

8   Have you not set mine honor at the stake,
     And baited it with all th'unmuzzled thoughts
     That tyrannous heart can think ?

9   To one of your receiving
     Enough is shown; a cypress, not a bosom,
     Hides my [poor] heart .

10   So let me hear you speak .

Olivia

1   y'are servant to the Count Orsino youth .

---

2   For him, I thinke not on him.:for his thoughts,
    Would they were blankes, rather than fill'd with me .

---

3 {†} {I bid} you never speake againe of him ;
    But would you undertake another suite
    I had rather heare you, to solicit that,
    [Then] Musicke from the spheares .

---

4   Give me leave, beseech you : I did send,
    After the last enchantment you did [heare],
    A Ring in chace of you .

5   So did I abuse
    My selfe, my servant, and I feare me you :
    Under your hard construction must I sit,
    To force that on you in a shamefull cunning
    Which you knew none of yours .

6   What might you think ?

7   Have you not set mine Honor at the stake,
    And baited it with all th'unmuzled thoughts
    That tyrannous heart can think ?

8   To one of your receiving
    Enough is shewne, a Cipresse, not a bosome,
    Hides my [ ] heart : so let me heare you speake

- the speech starts off intellectually with its opening rebuke (2/0, F #1)—and that's about the only time intellect has any part to play in it

- the denial of Orsino is completely emotional (0/2, F #2), and the emotions become even more apparent as Olivia suggests that Cesario woo for 'himself' (1/6 in just the four lines of F #3)—with both the final surround phrase denial of Orsino and her opening, the suggestion of Cesario undertaking 'another suite', heightened by the only emotional semicolon in the speech

- the fact that the high-ranking Olivia is abasing herself to whom she believes to be a lower status 'gentleman' is accentuated in that her request ' . Give me leave, beseech you : ' is doubly weighted by its being an unembellished surround-phrase: the calm thus indicated perhaps suggests Olivia is either unused to beseeching, or is deliberately trying to maintain an air of calm so as not to frighten/turn off Cesario any further—and certainly, in comparison with what came before the rest of this sentence, it is well under control (1/1, F #4)

- and after the somewhat emotional apology for abusing 'My selfe, my servant, and I feare me you' is offered (0/2, line two of F #5), so the attempt to get some form of response from Cesario is very carefully voiced despite the extraordinarily powerful images used (1/1 the last three lines of F #5 through to F #7, five and a half lines in all)—though not particularly successfully, for even the careful short mono-syllabic unembellished direct request for a reply 'What might you think?' (F #6) fails to elicit a reply

- finally, with no response to date, the emotional dam bursts and Olivia's last surround phrase ' : so let me heare you speake . ' is the culmination of all caution seemingly thrown to the wind (1/5 in the two and a half lines of F #8)

Alls Well That Ends Well

Hellen

Not my virginity yet :
between 1.1.165–186

Background: a direct response to Parrolles' somewhat startlingly bold approach "Are you meditating on virginity?"

Style: as part of a two handed scene

Where: somewhere in the house or grounds of Rossillion

To Whom: Parrolles

# of Lines: 20

Probable Timing: 1.00 minutes

Take note: When Hellen's refusal of Parrolles' rather obvious enticements comes, it comes with complete finality, the speech starting with the unembellished surround phrase ' . Not my virginity yet : '.

Hellen

1   Not my virginity yet :
    There shall your master have a thousand loves,
    A mother, and a mistress, and a friend,
    A phoenix, captain, and an enemy,
    A guide, a goddess, and a sovereign,
    A counsellor, a traitress, and a dear ;
    His humble ambition, proud humility ;
    His jarring, concord, and his discord, dulcet ;
    His faith, his sweet disaster ; with a world
    Of pretty fond adoptious christendoms
    That blinking Cupid gossips .

2   Now shall he -
    I know not what he shall—God send him well !

3   The court's a learning place, and he is one -

That I wish well .

4   'Tis pity—

That wishing well had not a body in't,
Which might be felt, that we, the poorer born,
Whose baser stars do shut us up in wishes,
Might with effects of them follow our friends,
And show what we alone must think, which never
Returns us thanks.

Hellen

1   Not my virginity yet :
      There shall your Master have a thousand loves,
      A Mother, and a Mistresse, and a friend,
      A Phenix, Captaine, and an enemy,
      A guide, a Goddesse, and a Soveraigne,
      A Counsellor, a Traitoresse, and a Deare :
      His humble ambition, proud humility :
      His jarring, concord : and his discord, dulcet :
      His faith, his sweet disaster : with a world
      Of pretty fond adoptious christendomes
      That blinking Cupid gossips .

2   Now shall he :
      I know not what he shall, God send him well,
      The Courts a learning place, and he is one,

      That I wish well .

3   'Tis pitty,

      That wishing well had not a body in't,
      Which might be felt, that we the poorer borne,
      Whose baser starres do shut us up in wishes,
      Might with effects of them follow our friends,
      And shew what we alone must thinke, which never
      Returnes us thankes .

- however, the thought(s) of Bertram becoming her first lover moves her into an entirely different mood

  a. first intellectual, as she lists in the next six lines all the different aspects of her femininity she could present him (10/6)

  b. and this then moves her into five consecutive surround phrases as she imagines what effect this would have on him and how he would respond, the reverie being incredibly quiet for the first four unembellished surround phrases, as if she didn't want to break the magic of the dream she is weaving, with only the last finally breaking into a little passion (1/1, the last two lines of F #1)

- the slightly onrushed F #2 points to the probable awkwardness she experiences when her Bertram-reverie finally breaks, for after what seems to build to yet another wonderful moment of imagination (the opening unembellished surround phrase of F #2, ' . Now shall he : '), her attempt at some form of intellectual recovery (2/0, the remainder of F #2) is more than somewhat undermined by both the ensuing content and the ungrammatical fast-link comma ending F #2's second line (this attempts to connect two totally different ideas, the already peculiar non-sequitur of 'I know not' coupled with her good wishes for Bertram, being tacked onto an irrelevant comment about 'The Courts a learning place', with one more peculiar illogical—and unfinished—switch back to Bertram 'and he is one')

- her final attempt to explain to the presumably now totally befuddled (yet perhaps even more aroused) Parrolles that it would be nice if wishes could become reality, is, for the first time in the speech, totally emotional (0/6)—(personal embarrassment at how much of herself she has revealed in the earlier part of the speech perhaps?)

Alls Well That Ends Well

Hellen

Then I confesse/Here on my knee, high and you,
1.3.191–217

Background: pushed very hard by the Countesse, Hellen at last tells the Countesse of her impossible love for the Countesse's son, Bertram.

Style: as part of a two handed scene

Where: somewhere in the house of Rossillion

To Whom: Bertram's mother, the Countesse

# of Lines: 26

Probable Timing: 1.15 minutes

Take note: F's sentence structure suggests that, though Hellen may be uncomfortable at the top of the speech, especially with the onrush of F #1 and the very ungrammatical period that ends it, she manages to harness her thinking, if not her emotions, to a more rational flow by the speech's end. And though she attempts to start carefully, the four semicolons scattered through the speech suggests that there are times where the strength of her love for Bertram almost runs away with her.

Hellen

1   Then I confess
Here on my knee, before high heaven and you,
That before you , and next unto high heaven,
I love your son .

2   My friends were poor, but honest, so's my love .

3   Be not offended, for it hurts not him
That he is lov'd of me ; I follow him not
By any token of presumptuous suit,
Nor would I have him till I do deserve him,
Yet never know how that desert should be .

4   I know I love in vain, strive against hope ;
Yet in this captious, and [untenable] sieve
I still pour in the waters of my love
And lack not to lose still .

5   Thus Indian-like,
Religious in mine error, I adore
The sun, that looks upon his worshipper,
But knows of him no more .

6   My dearest madam,
Let not your hate encounter with my love
For loving where you do ; but if yourself,
Whose aged honor cites a virtuous youth,
Did ever, in so true a flame of liking
Wish chastely, and love dearly, that your Dian
Was both herself and love, O then give pity
To her whose state is such, that cannot choose
But lend and give where she is sure to lose;
That seeks not to find that her search implies,
But riddle like lives sweetly where she dies .

Hellen

1 Then I confesse
   Here on my knee, before high heaven and you,
   That before you, and next unto high heaven, I love your
      Sonne :
   My friends were poore but honest, so's my love :
   Be not offended, for it hurts not him
   That he is lov'd of me ; I follow him not
   By any token of presumptuous suite,
   Nor would I have him, till I doe deserve him,
   Yet never know how that desert should be :
   I know I love in vaine, strive against hope :
   Yet in this captious, and [intemible] Sive .

2 I still poure in the waters of my love
   And lacke not to loose still ; thus Indian like
   Religious in mine error, I adore
   The Sunne that lookes upon his worshipper,
   But knowes of him no more .

3   My deerest Madam,
   Let not your hate incounter with my love,
   For loving where you doe ; but if your selfe,
   Whose aged honor cites a vertuous youth,
   Did ever, in so true a flame of liking,
   Wish chastly, and love dearely, that your Dian
   Was both her selfe and love, O then give pittie
   To her whose state is such, that cannot choose
   But lend and give where she is sure to loose ;
   That seekes not to finde that, her search implies,
   But riddle like, lives sweetely where she dies .

- after the release of 'confesse' in the opening line (the key to the whole speech), her attempt to control the, to her, awful confirmation of aiming above her station by loving the Countesse's son, lasts for almost two unembellished lines—the attempt blown apart by the second line being fourteen syllables long, and the veritable explosion of the final admission of whom she loves, 'your Sonne.'

- the very few surround phrases point to the emotional tug of war Hellen is suffering—first as to her own worth

    " : My friends were poore but honest, so's my love : " then as to her chances of success

    " : I know I love in vaine, strive against hope : /Yet in this captious, and intemible Sive . /I still poure in the waters of my love/And lacke not to loose still ; "

and the depth of feeling here is underscored by what most modern texts regard as a dreadful period after 'Sive', and they remove all punctuation to allow the idea to flow on unchecked: however, F's totally ungrammatical period allows Hellen a long moment of recovery from the appalling image of her never-ending loss before continuing with F #2—and indeed this moment seems to mark where the nature of her speech markedly changes

- overall, the speech has opened somewhat emotionally (2/6, the first ten lines of F #1, to this ungrammatical point), but after the seemingly much needed (yet modern texts denied) period, the releases start to flow much more heavily

- F #2's opening imagery of her still pouring in 'the waters of my love' is out and out emotional (0/3 in one and a half lines), followed by passion as she describes her behaviour as 'Religious in mine error' (2/3, the remaining three and a half lines of F #2)—and the last long flowing sentence appealing for empathy and understanding is again almost completely emotional (3/10 in F #3's ten and a half lines)

Alls Well That Ends Well

Diana

When midnight comes, knocke at my chamber window:
between 4.254–76

Background: Diana appears to acquiesce to Bertram's seductive pleadings, though once he leaves she makes it very clear just what has been going on (a definite victory for the chaste huntress it would seem).

Style: initially as part of a two-handed scene, and then solo

Where: unspecified, but presumably somewhere in or near Diana's home

To Whom: Bertram, and then direct audience address

# of Lines: 20

Probable Timing: 1.00 minutes

Take note: Once more Diana's skilful use of calmness is evident, this time as a stunning seduction technique, as is the long tantalising sexual build-up of onrushed F #2.

Diana

1   When midnight comes, knock at my cham-
         ber window ;
     I'll order take my mother shall not hear .

2   Now will I charge you in the band of truth,
     When you have conquered my yet-maiden bed,
     Remain there but an hour, nor speak to me .

3   My reasons are most strong, and you shall know them
     When back again this ring shall be deliver'd ;
     And on your finger in the night, I'll put
     Another ring, that what in time proceeds
     May token to the future, our past deeds .

4   Adieu till then, then fail not .

5   You have won
     A wife of me, though there my hope be done .

---

6   My mother told me just how he would woo,
     As if she sate in's heart .

7   She says, all men
     Have the like oaths .

8   He [has] sworn to marry me
     When his wife's dead ; therefore I'll lie with him
     When I am buried .

9   Since Frenchmen are so braid,
     Marry that will, I live and die a maid .

10   Only in this disguise I think't no sin
     To cozen him that would unjustly win

Diana

1 When midnight comes, knocke at my cham-
          ber window :
    Ile order take, my mother shall not heare .

2 Now will I charge you in the band of truth,
    When you have conquer'd my yet maiden-bed,
    Remaine there but an houre, nor speake to mee :
    My reasons are most strong, and you shall know them,
    When backe againe this Ring shall be deliver'd :
    And on your finger in the night, Ile put
    Another Ring, that what in time proceeds,
    May token to the future, our past deeds .

3 Adieu till then, then faile not : you have wonne
    A wife of me, though there my hope be done .

---

4 My mother told me just how he would woo,
    As if she sate in's heart .

5   She sayes, all men
    Have the like oathes : He [had] sworne to marrie me
    When his wife's dead : therfore Ile lye with him
    When I am buried .

6   Since Frenchmen are so braide,
    Marry that will, I live and die a Maid :
    Onely in this disguise,   I think't no sinne,
    To cosen him that would unjustly winne .

- thus the opening assignation time-setting 'When midnight comes' is unembellished, as is the strength of the suggestion that they will not be disturbed 'Ile order take', which leads to the two line unembellished enticement

  " Now will I charge you in the band of truth,/When you have conquer'd my yet maiden-bed,"

- the clever unembellished suggestion of games within games, that she'll put a 'Ring'

  "And on your finger in the night,...that what in time proceeds, / May token to the future, our past deeds ."

is brilliantly understated, in that at one and the same time it ensures the bed-trick will actually work, for Bertram will have given up his own ring which the actual bed-partner Hellen will need as part of his challenge to her that she must obtain before he will acknowledge her as his wife, while at the same time fooling Bertram into concentrating on the physicality of the evening's forthcoming pleasures

- while Diana's unembellished build to her final beguilement

  " . Adieu till then, then faile not : you have wonne/A wife of me, though there my hope be done . "

is utterly brilliant, its enticements heightened by being made up of two surround phrases too

- as with the previous speech, small bursts of emotion do shake Diana's outward calm at times, as with the instructions to "remaine there but an houre, nor speake to mee' (0/4 in one line); that supposedly his own ring will be returned 'backe againe' (which it won't); the rhyme of the speech ending justification of deceiving him, 'sinne'/'winne'

- once the besotted and aroused Bertram leaves, the enormous depth of her convictions are shown by the only remaining unembellished line 'My mother told me just how he would woo" and by the three final dismissive surround phrases totally forming F #5

- thus it's not surprising that overall, amid the moments of needed and skilful self-control, Diana's releases in the speech are essentially emotional (5/19 in twenty lines)

The Winter's Tale

Hermione

What ? have I twice said well ? when was't before ?
between 1.2.90 = 106

Background: daughter of the 'Emperor of Russia', married to Leontes King of Sicilia, has publicly and with no difficulty whatsoever very quickly managed to persuade Polixenes, King of Bohemia, a close boyhood friend of her husband, to stay at the Sicilian court a week longer, even though Leontes had been unable to do so. The following is her response to Leontes 'thou never spoak'st/To better purpose.', which he has immediately modified with his further 'Never, but once'.

Style: one on one in front of a small group, and perhaps a larger group in the background

Where: somewhere in the palace of Sicilia

To Whom: her husband Leontes, in front of Polixenes, Camillo (Leontes' key advisor), Mamillius (her son), and perhaps members of both courts

# of Lines: 15

Probable Timing: 0.50 minutes

Take note: In such a pleasant social situation, the plethora of surround phrases seem to suggest a character who is enjoying herself thoroughly in teasing and challenging all around her, especially her husband Leontes.

Hermione

1   What ? have I twice said well ?

2   When was't before ?

3   I prithee tell me ; cram's with praise, and make's
    As fat as tame things .

4   One good deed, dying tongueless
    Slaughters a thousand, waiting upon that .

5   Our praises are our wages .

6   You may ride's
    With one soft kiss a thousand furlongs ere
    With spur we heat an acre .

7   But to th'goal :
    My last good deed, was to entreat his stay ;
    What was my first ?

8   It has an elder sister,
    Or I mistake you .

9   O, would her name were Grace !

10 But once before I spoke to th'purpose ? when ?

11 Nay, let me have't ; I long .

---

12 Why lo you now !

13   I have spoke to th'purpose twice :
    The one, for ever earn'd a royal husband ;
    Th'other, for some while a friend .

Hermione

1   What ? have I twice said well ? when was't before ?

2   I prethee tell me : cram's with prayse, and make's
    As fat as tame things : One good deed, dying tonguelesse,
    Slaughters a thousand, wayting upon that .

3   Our prayses are our Wages .

4   You may ride's
    With one soft Kisse a thousand Furlongs, ere
    With Spur we heat an Acre .

5   But to th'Goale :
    My last good deed, was to entreat his stay .

6   What was my first ? it ha's an elder Sister,
    Or I mistake you : O, would her Name were Grace .

7   But once before I spoke to th'purpose ? when ?

8   Nay, let me have't : I long .

---

9   Why lo-you now ; I have spoke to th'purpose twice :
    The one, for ever earn'd a Royall Husband ;
    Th'other, for some while a Friend .

- Hermione's lively mind and spirit can be seen throughout

  a. from the easy unembellished but persistent surround phrase opening of F #1 and the first phrase of F #2 leading to ' I prethee tell me : '

  b. through the logical unembellished surround phrases of F #5-6 starting with ' . But to th'Goale : '

  c. to the (delighted?) finale of F #9 including ' ; I have spoke to th'purpose twice : '

- while the speech starts fairly easily (0/1, the first two and a half lines), Hermione soon allows releases to begin, enjoying herself perhaps?, (1/2, the one and a half lines ending F #2)

- the shortness of F #3's 'Our prayses are our Wages.' suggests that she really does enjoy public approval, for the explanation of a 'Kisse' being better encouragement than a 'Spur' is splendidly intellectual (4/1, F #4)

- once she embarks on her mission to discover when was the first time she 'said well', emotions seem to have no place, for in her single-mindedness the remainder of the speech becomes a mixture of short sentences (F #7 and #8) unembellished phrases (ten), surround phrases (eleven), and intellect (8/2 in eight and a half lines, F #5-9)

- and though there is one emotional release in the final stage (the accurate and yet lovely assessment of her husband as 'Royall'), the s of the final sentence suggest that there is a great deal of pleasure in her pursuit

The Winter's Tale

Hermione

Sir, spare your Threats :
3.2.91–116

Background: as the court battle reaches its climax, the following is Hermione's direct response to Leontes, triggered by his unequivocal final remark, 'so thou/Shalt feele our Justice; in whose easiest passage,/Looke for no lesse then death'.

Style: essentially one on one, via public address until the last sentence, which is directed towards the larger group

Where: in open court

To Whom: Leontes, in front of the full assembly—with all present being addressed in the final sentence

# of Lines: 26

Probable Timing: 1.15 minutes

Take Note: A wonderful indication of Hermione's nobility and strength of character is the way that she handles her personal grief in such a quiet unembellished manner, the needed facts for all to understand not giving way to unseemly emotion. And that the listing of her third discomfort leads to two further separate sentences spelling all that has happened to her (F #4-5) instead of being lumped in as part of her third grief (mt. #5) suggests a formidable intellect at work despite the pain.

Hermione

1 Sir, spare your threats .
2 The bug which you would fright me with, I seek.
3 To me can life be no commodity ;
   The crown and comfort of my life, your favor,
   I do give lost, for I do feel it gone,
   But know not how it went .
4   My second joy,
   And first fruits of my body, from his presence
   I am barr'd, like one infectious .
5   My third comfort
   (Starr'd most unluckily) is from my breast
   (The innocent milk in it most innocent mouth)
   Hal'd out to murther ;myself on every post
   Proclaim'd a strumpet ; with immodest hatred
   The childbed privilege denied, which 'longs
   To women of all fashion ; lastly, hurried
   Here to this place, i'th'open air, before
   I have got strength of limit .
6   Now, my liege,
   Tell me what blessings I have here alive,
   That I should fear to die ?
7   Therefore proceed .
8 But yet hear this—mistake me not ; no life,
   (I prize it not a straw) but for mine honor,
   Which I would free—if I shall be condemn'd
   Upon surmises (all proofs sleeping else
   But what your jealousies awake), I tell you
   'Tis rigor and not law .
9   Your honors all,
   I do refer me to the oracle :
   Apollo be my judge !

Hermione

1 Sir, spare your Threats :
   The Bugge which you would fright me with, I seeke :
   To me can Life be no commoditie ;
   The crowne and comfort of my Life (your Favor)
   I doe give lost, for I doe feele it gone,
   But know not how it went .

2   My second Joy,
   And first Fruits of my body, from his presence
   I am bar'd, like one infectious .

3   My third comfort
   (Star'd most unluckily) is from my breast
   (The innocent milke in it most innocent mouth)
   Hal'd out to murther .

4   My selfe on every Post
   Proclaym'd a Strumpet : With immodest hatred
   The Child-bed priviledge deny'd, which longs
   To Women of all fashion .

5   Lastly, hurried
   Here, to this place, i'th'open ayre, before
   I have got strength of limit .

6   Now (my Liege)
   Tell me what blessings I have here alive,
   That I should feare to die ?

7   Therefore proceed :
   But yet heare this : mistake me not : no Life,
   (I prize it not a straw) but for mine Honor,
   Which I would free : if I shall be condemn'd
   Upon surmizes (all proofes sleeping else,
   But what your Jealousies awake) I tell you
   'Tis Rigor and not Law .

8   Your Honors all,
   I doe referre me to the Oracle :
   Apollo be my Judge .

- though onrushed, Hermione's opening put-down of Leontes' less than rational response is superbly absolute; passionate (3/2, the first three lines of F #1); driven home by three successive surround phrases; though there is obviously some emotion lurking underneath, the last surround phrase finishing with a

- of the unembellished phrases, the first gives stark recognition to the grief that her acknowledged loss of what were her three greatest 'comforts' are causing her,

  a. from the first mention of the loss of her husband's love, via the monosyllabic end of F #1, 'But know not how it went.'

  b. then as regards her beloved son
      " . . from his presence/I am bar'd, like one infectious."

  c. and the loss of her new-born baby daughter
      "My third comfort/(Star'd most unluckily) is from my breast/ . . . /Hal'd out to murther"

      and then she turns to her physical state
      "Lastly, hurried/Here, to this place . . . before/I have got strength of limit."

      followed by the direct public challenge to her husband/judge
      "Now . . . /Tell me what blessings I have here alive, . . . Therefore proceed:"

- but in the midst of her personal grief she never loses sight of what is essential, as the surround phrase strength with which she so firmly points out to the assembled crowd how badly her reputation has been impugned testifies
    " . My selfe on every Post/Proclaym'd a Strumpet : "

- the speech is a mixture of unembellished lines with intellect usually dominating emotion (22/18 overall), with the only emotional passage the public acknowledgement of the loss of Leontes' love (2/4, the last three lines of F #1), and the only moment of almost matched intellectual and emotional release in F #4's delineation of how badly she has been treated both in reputation, being 'Proclaym'd a Strumpet', and in having her 'Child-bed priviledge deny'd' (5/4)

The Tempest

Miranda

I do not know/One of my sexe ; no womans face remember,
between 3.1.48–86

Background: and this is Miranda's response to Ferdinand's love declaration. Since she has had no experience of playing coy (compare
Juliet's lovely admission to Romeo, 'I should have beene more
strange, I must confesse'), she is as innocently open, direct, and
honest as she is elsewhere in the play.

Style: as part of a two-handed scene

Where: near to Prospero's cell

To Whom: Ferdinand unaware that Prospero is watching

# of Lines: 21

Probable Timing: 1.10 minutes

Take note: In comparison to most modern texts' rational nine sentences, F's five sentences seem to present a character with much
less self-control—yet by speech's end, F's orthography has marked
Miranda's wonderful growth from awkwardness to maturity—a
far more interesting and truthful human reality for a young ado-
lescent in love than the self-controlled young woman the modern
reworking seems to present.

Miranda

1   I do not know
     One of my se ; no woman's face remember,
     Save, from my glass, mine own; nor have I seen
     More that I may call men [than] you, good friend,
     And my dear father .

2   How features are abroad
     I am skilless of ; but by my modesty
     (The jewel in my dower), I would not wish
     Any companion in the world but you ;
     Nor can imagination form a shape,
     Besides your self, to like of .

3   But I prattle
     Something too wildly, and my father's precepts
     I therein do forget .

---

4   I am a fool
     To weep at what I am glad of .

---

5   {And I weep }
     At mine unworthiness, that dare not offer
     What I desire to give, and much less take
     What I shall die to want .

6   But this is trifling;
     And all the more it seeks to hide itself,
     The bigger bulk it shows .

7   Hence, bashful cunning!
     And prompt me, plain and holy innocence !

8   I am your wife, if you will marry me ;
     If not, I'll die your maid .

9   To be your fellow
     You may deny me ; but I'll be your servant,
     Whether you will or no .

Miranda

1   I do not know
    One of my sexe ; no womans face remember,
    Save from my glasse, mine owne : Nor have I seene
    More that I may call men, [then] you good friend,
    And my deere Father : how features are abroad
    I am skillesse of ; but by my modestie
    (The jewell in my dower) I would not wish
    Any Companion in the world but you :
    Nor can imagination forme a shape
    Besides your selfe, to like of : but I prattle
    Something too wildely, and my Fathers precepts
    I therein do forget .

---

2   I am a foole
    To weepe at what I am glad of .

---

3   {And I weepe }
    At mine unworthinesse, that dare not offer
    What I desire to give ; and much lesse take
    What I shall die to want : But this is trifling,
    And all the more it seekes to hide it selfe,
    The bigger bulke it shewes .

4   Hence bashfull cunning,
    And prompt me plaine and holy innocence .

5   I am your wife, if you will marrie me ;
    If not, Ile die your maid : to be your fellow
    You may denie me, but Ile be your servant
    Whether you will or no .

- that Miranda finds her I-don't-know-what-men-and-women-are-like opening quite awkward can be seen in that

  a. F sets the confession as one onrushed sentence

  b. there are four pieces of major punctuation in the first five lines

  c. three of the four surround phrases so created are emotional, formed in part by semicolons

  d. the whole is quite emotional (2/6)

- and, as she asserts by the 'jewell' of her 'modestie' she 'would not wish/Any Companion in the world but you', she seems to establish self-control, for in the ensuing four lines only three operative words are singled out for release, (as already seen 'jewell' and 'Companion', accompanied by 'your selfe'), all three vital to her own declaration of love, the latter heightened by being set in a surround phrase

- and, as charmingly as with Ferdinand's awkwardness, her confession that she prattles 'Something too wildely' is also set as a surround phrase where emotion and intellect both break into her self-control (1/1, the last two lines of F #1)

- and then her emotions take over a she voices thoughts of her own 'unworthinesse' and acknowledges her tears (1/9, F #2-3)—especially noticeable in the only (emotional) surround phrase in the sentence, ' ; and much lesse take/What I shall die to want ; '—its pain heightened by being monosyllabic

- yet, a great testament to her inner fortitude, following her emotional rejection of 'bashfull cunning' and her plea for the help of 'holy innocence' (F #4, 0/2), the final three and half line declaration of complete love is totally unembellished, the first declarations once more formed by two emotional surround phrases

BIBLIOGRAPHY

AND

APPENDICES

BIBLIOGRAPHY

The most easily accessible general information is to be found under the citations of *Campbell,* and of *Halliday.* The finest summation of matters academic is to be found within the all-encompassing *A Textual Companion,* listed below in the first part of the bibliography under *Wells, Stanley and Taylor, Gary* (eds.)

Individual modern editions consulted are listed below under the separate headings 'The Complete Works in Compendium Format' and 'The Complete Works in Separate Individual Volumes,' from which the modern text audition speeches have been collated and compiled.

All modern act, scene, and/or line numbers refer the reader to *The Riverside Shakespeare,* in my opinion still the best of the complete works, despite the excellent compendiums that have been published since.

The F/Q material is taken from a variety of already published sources, including not only all the texts listed in the 'Photostatted Reproductions in Compendium Format' below, but also earlier individually printed volumes, such as the twentieth century editions published under the collective title *The Facsimiles of Plays from The First Folio of Shakespeare* by Faber & Gwyer, and the nineteenth century editions published on behalf of The New Shakespere Society.

The heading 'Single Volumes of Special Interest' is offered to newcomers to Shakespeare in the hope that the books may add useful knowledge about the background and craft of this most fascinating of theatrical figures.

PHOTOSTATTED REPRODUCTIONS OF THE ORIGINAL TEXTS IN COMPENDIUM FORMAT

Allen, M.J.B. and K. Muir, (eds.). *Shakespeare's Plays in Quarto.* Berkeley: University of California Press, 1981.

Blaney, Peter (ed.). *The Norton Facsimile (The First Folio of Shakespeare).* New York: W.W.Norton & Co., Inc., 1996 (see also Hinman, below).

Brewer D.S. (ed.). *Mr. William Shakespeare's Comedies, Histories & Tragedies, The Second/Third/Fourth Folio Reproduced in Facsimile.* (3 vols.), 1983.

Hinman, Charlton (ed.). *The Norton Facsimile (The First Folio of Shakespeare)*. New York: W.W.Norton & Company, Inc., 1968.

Kokeritz, Helge (ed.). *Mr. William Shakespeare 's Comedies, Histories & Tragedies*. New Haven: Yale University Press, 1954.

Moston, Doug (ed.). *Mr. William Shakespeare's Comedies, Histories, and Tragedies*. New York: Routledge, 1998.

MODERN TYPE VERSION OF THE FIRST FOLIO IN COMPENDIUM FORMAT

Freeman, Neil. (ed.). *The Applause First Folio of Shakespeare in Modern Type*. New York & London: Applause Books, 2001.

MODERN TEXT VERSIONS OF THE COMPLETE WORKS IN COMPENDIUM FORMAT

Craig, H. and D. Bevington (eds.). *The Complete Works of Shakespeare*. Glenview: Scott, Foresman and Company, 1973.

Evans, G.B. (ed.). *The Riverside Shakespeare*. Boston: Houghton Mifflin Company, 1974.

Wells, Stanley and Gary Taylor (eds.). *The Oxford Shakespeare, William Shakespeare , the Complete Works, Original Spelling Edition,* Oxford: The Clarendon Press, 1986.

Wells, Stanley and Gary Taylor (eds.). *The Oxford Shakespeare, William Shakespeare, The Complete Works, Modern Spelling Edition.* Oxford: The Clarendon Press, 1986.

MODERN TEXT VERSIONS OF THE COMPLETE WORKS IN SEPARATE INDIVIDUAL VOLUMES

The Arden Shakespeare. London: Methuen & Co. Ltd., Various dates, editions, and editors .

Folio Texts. Freeman, Neil H. M. (ed.) Applause First Folio Editions, 1997, and following.

The New Cambridge Shakespeare. Cambridge: Cambridge University Press. Various dates, editions, and editors.

New Variorum Editions of Shakespeare. Furness, Horace Howard (original editor.). New York: 1880, Various reprints. All these volumes have been in a state of re-editing and reprinting since they first appeared in 1880. Various dates, editions, and editors.

The Oxford Shakespeare. Wells, Stanley (general editor). Oxford: Oxford University Press, Various dates and editors.

The New Penguin Shakespeare . Harmondsworth, Middlesex: Penguin Books, Various dates and editors.

The Shakespeare Globe Acting Edition. Tucker, Patrick and Holden, Michael. (eds.). London: M.H.Publications, Various dates.

SINGLE VOLUMES OF SPECIAL INTEREST

Baldwin, T.W. *William Shakespeare's Petty School*. 1943.

Baldwin, T.W. *William Shakespeare's Small wtin and Lesse Greeke*. (2 vols.) 1944.

Barton, John. *Playing Shakespeare*. 1984.

Beckerman, Bernard. *Shakespeare at the Globe, I 599-1609*. 1962. Berryman, John. *Berryman 's Shakespeare*. 1999.

Bloom, Harold. *Shakespeare: The Invention of the Human*. 1998. Booth, Stephen (ed.). *Shakespeare's Sonnets*. 1977.

Briggs, Katharine. *An Encyclopedia of Fairies*. 1976.

Campbell, Oscar James, and Edward G. Quinn (eds.). *The Reader's Encyclopedia of Shakespeare*. 1966.

Crystal, David, and Ben Crystal. *Shakespeare's Words: A Glossary & Language Companion*. 2002.

Flatter, Richard. *Shakespeare's Producing Hand*. 1948 (reprint).

Ford, Boris. (ed.). *The Age of Shakespeare*. 1955.

Freeman, Neil H.M. *Shakespeare's First Texts*. 1994.

Greg, W.W. *The Editorial Problem in Shakespeare: A Survey of the Foundations of the Text*. 1954 (3rd. edition).

Gurr, Andrew . *Playgoing in Shakespeare's London*. 1987. Gurr, Andrew. *The Shakespearean Stage, 1574-1642*. 1987. Halliday, F.E. *A Shakespeare Companion*. 1952.

Harbage, Alfred. *Shakespeare's Audience*. 1941.

Harrison, G.B. (ed.). *The Elizabethan Journals*. 1965 (revised, 2 vols.).

Harrison, G.B. (ed.). *A Jacobean Journal*. 1941.

Harrison, G.B. (ed.). *A Second Jacobean Journal*. 1958.

Hinman, Charlton. *The Printing and Proof Reading of the First Folio of Shakespeare*. 1963 (2 vols.).

Joseph, Bertram. *Acting Shakespeare*. 1960.

Joseph, Miriam (Sister). *Shakespeare's Use of The Arts of wnguage*.1947.

King, T.J. *Casting Shakespeare's Plays*. 1992.

Lee, Sidney and C.T. Onions. *Shakespeare's England : An Account Of The Life And Manners Of His Age*. (2 vols.) 1916.

Linklater, Kristin. *Freeing Shakespeare's Voice.* 1992.

Mahood, **M .M.** *Shakespeare's Wordplay.* 1957.

O'Connor, Gary. *William Shakespeare: A Popular Life.* 2000.

Ordish, T.F. *Early London Theatres.* 1894. (1971 reprint).

Rodenberg, Patsy. *Speaking Shakespeare.* 2002.

Schoenbaum. S. *William Shakespeare: A Documentary Life.* 1975.

Shapiro, Michael. *Children of the Revels.* 1977.

Simpson, Percy. *Shakespeare's Punctuation.* 1969 (reprint).

Smith, Irwin. *Shakespeare's Blackfriars Playhouse .* 1964.

Southern, Richard. *The Staging of Plays Before Shakespeare.* 1973.

Spevack, M. *A Complete and Systematic Concordance to the Works Of Shakespeare .* 1968-1980 (9vols.).

Tillyard, E.M.W. *The Elizabethan World Picture.* 1942.

Trevelyan, G.M. (ed.). *Illustrated English Social History.* 1942.

Vendler, Helen. *The Art of Shakespeare's Sonnets.* 1999.

Walker, Alice F. *Textual Problems of the First Folio.* 1953.

Walton, J.K. *The Quarto Copy of the First Folio.* 1971.

Warren, Michael. *William Shakespeare, The Parallel King Lear 1608-1623.*

Wells, Stanley and Taylor, Gary (eds.). *Modernising Shakespeare's Spelling, with Three Studies in The Text of Henry V.* 1975.

Wells, Stanley. *Re-Editing Shakespeare for the Modern Reader.* 1984.

Wells, Stanley and Gary Taylor (eds.). *William Shakespeare: A Textual Companion .* 1987.

Wright, George T. *Shakespeare's Metrical Art.* 1988.

HISTORICAL DOCUMENTS

Daniel, Samuel. *The Fowre Bookes of the Civile Warres Between The Howses Of Lancaster and Yorke.* 1595.

Holinshed, Raphael. *Chronicles of England, Scotland and Ireland.* 1587 (2nd. edition).

Halle, Edward. *The Union of the Two Noble and Illustre Famelies of Lancastre And Yorke.* 1548 (2nd. edition).

Henslowe, Philip: Foakes, R.A. and Rickert (eds.). *Henslowe's Diary.* 1961.

Plutarch: North, Sir Thomas (translation of a work in French prepared by Jacques Amyots). *The Lives of The Noble Grecians and Romanes.* 1579.

APPENDIX 1:
GUIDE TO THE EARLY TEXTS

A QUARTO (Q)

A single text, so called because of the book size resulting from a particular method of printing. Eighteen of Shakespeare's plays were published in this format by different publishers at various dates between 1594-1622, prior to the appearance of the 1623 Folio.

THE FIRST FOLIO (F1)'

Thirty-six of Shakespeare's plays (excluding *Pericles* and *Two Noble Kinsmen,* in which he had a hand) appeared in one volume, published in 1623. All books of this size were termed Folios, again because of the sheet size and printing method, hence this volume is referred to as the First Folio. For publishing details see Bibliography, 'Photostated Reproductions of the Original Texts.'

THE SECOND FOLIO (F2)

Scholars suggest that the Second Folio, dated 1632 but perhaps not published until 1640, has little authority, especially since it created hundreds of new problematic readings of its own. Nevertheless more than 800 modern text readings can be attributed to it. The **Third Folio** (1664) and the **Fourth Folio** (1685) have even less authority, and are rarely consulted except in cases of extreme difficulty.

APPENDIX 2:
WORD, WORDS, WORDS

PART ONE: VERBAL CONVENTIONS (AND HOW THEY WILL BE SET IN THE FOLIO TEXT)

"THEN" AND "THAN"

These two words, though their neutral vowels sound different to modern ears, were almost identical to Elizabethan speakers and readers, despite their different meanings. F and Q make little distinction between them, setting them interchangeably . The original setting will be used, and the modern reader should soon get used to substituting one for the other as necessary.

"I," "AY," AND "AYE"

F/Q often print the personal pronoun "I" and the word of agreement "aye" simply as "I." Again, the modern reader should quickly get used to this and make the substitution when necess ary. The reader should also be aware that very occasionally either word could be used and the phrase make perfect sense, even though different meanings would be implied.

"MY SELFE/HIM SELFE/HER SELFE" VERSUS "MYSELF/HIMSELF/HER-SELF"

Generally F/Q separate the two parts of the word, "my selfe" while most modern texts set the single word "myself." The difference is vital, based on Elizabethan philosophy. Elizabethans regarded themselves as composed of two parts, the corporeal "I," and the more spiritual part, the "self." Thus, when an Elizabethan character refers to "my selfe," he or she is often referring to what is to all intents and purposes a separate being, even if that being is a particular part of him- or herself. Thus soliloquies can be thought of as a debate between the "I" and "my selfe," and, in such speeches, even though there may be only one character on-stage, it's as if there were two distinct entities present.

UNUSUAL SPELLING OF REAL NAMES, BOTH OF PEOPLE AND PLACES

Real names, both of people and places, and foreign languages are often reworked for modern understanding. For example, the French town often set in Fl as "Callice" is usually reset as "Calais." F will be set as is.

NON-GRAMMATICAL USES OF VERBS IN BOTH TENSE AND APPLICATION

Modern texts 'correct' the occasional Elizabethan practice of setting a singular noun with plural verb (and vice versa), as well as the infrequent use of the past tense of a verb to describe a current situation. The F reading will be set as is, without annotation.

ALTERNATIVE SETTINGS OF A WORD WHERE DIFFERENT SPELLINGS MAINTAIN THE SAME MEANING

F/Q occasionally set what appears to modern eyes as an archaic spelling of a word for which there is a more common modern alternative, for example "murther" for murder , "burthen" for burden, "moe" for more, "vilde" for vile. Though some modern texts set the Fl (or alternative Q) setting, others modernise. Fl will be set as is with no annotation.

ALTERNATIVE SETTINGS OF A WORD WHERE DIFFERENT SPELLINGS SUGGEST DIFFERENT MEANINGS

Far more complicated is the situation where, while an Elizabethan could substitute one word formation for another and still imply the same thing, to modern eyes the substituted word has an entirely different meaning to the one it has replaced. The following is by no means an exclusive list of the more common dual-spelling, dual-meaning words

anticke-antique	mad-made	sprite-spirit
born-borne	metal-mettle	sun-sonne
hart-heart	mote-moth	travel-travaill
human-humane	pour-(po wre)-power	through-thorough
lest-least	reverent-reverend	troth-truth
lose-loose	right-rite	whether-whither

Some of these doubles offer a metrical problem too, for example "sprite," a one syllable word, versus "spirit." A potential problem occurs in *A Midsummer Nights Dream,* where the modern text s set Q1's "thorough," and thus the scansion pattern of elegant magic can be established, whereas F1's more plebeian "through" sets up a much more awkward and clumsy moment.

The F reading will be set in the Folio Text, as will the modern texts' substitution of a different word formation in the Modern Text. If the modern text substitution has the potential to alter the meaning (and sometimes scansion) of the line, it will be noted accordingly.

PART TWO: WORD FORMATIONS COUNTED AS EQUIVALENTS FOR THE FOLLOWING SPEECHES

Often the spelling differences between the original and modern texts are quite obvious, as with "she"/"shee". And sometimes Folio text passages are so flooded with longer (and sometimes shorter) spellings that, as described in the General Introduction, it would seem that vocally something unusual is taking place as the character speaks.

However, there are some words where the spelling differences are so marginal that they need not be explored any further. The following is by no mean s an exclusive list of word s that in the main will not be taken into account when discussing emotional moments in the various commentaries accompanying the audition speeches.

(modern text spelling shown first)

and- &	murder - murther	tabor - taber
apparent - apparant	mutinous - mutenous	ta'en - tane
briars - briers	naught - nought	then - than
choice - choise	obey - obay	theater - theatre
defense - defence	o'er - o're	uncurrant - uncurrent
debtor - debter	offense - offence	than - then
enchant - inchant	quaint - queint	venomous - venemous
endurance - indurance	reside - recide	virtue - vertue
ere - e'er	Saint - S.	weight - waight
expense - expence	sense - sence	
has - ha's	sepulchre - sepulcher	
heinous - hainous	show - shew	
I'11 - Ile	solicitor - soliciter	
increase - encrease	sugar - suger	

APPENDIX 3:
THE PATTERN OF MAGIC, RITUAL &
INCANTATION

THE PATTERNS OF "NORMAL" CONVERSATION

The normal pattern of a regular Shakespearean verse line is akin to five pairs of human heart beats, with ten syllables being arranged in five pairs of beats, each pair alternating a pattern of a weak stress followed by a strong stress. Thus, a normal ten syllable heartbeat line (with the emphasis on the capitalised words) would read as

weak- STRONG, weak - STRONG, weak- STRONG, weak- STRONG, weak- STRONG
(shall   I   com-   PARE thee   TO   a   SUMM- ers DAY)

Breaks would either be in length (under or over ten syllables) or in rhythm (any combinations of stresses other than the five pairs of weak-strong as shown above), or both together.

THE PATTERNS OF MAGIC, RITUAL, AND INCANTATION

Whenever magic is used in the Shakespeare plays the form of the spoken verse changes markedly in two ways . The length is usually reduced from ten to just seven syllables, and the pattern of stresses is completely reversed, as if the heartbeat was being forced either by the circumstances of the scene or by the need of the speaker to completely change direction. Thus in comparison to the normal line shown above, or even the occasional minor break, the more tortured and even dangerous magic or ritual line would read as

    STRONG - weak, STRONG- weak, STRONG - weak, STRONG
    (WHEN shall WE   three   MEET   a   GAINE)

The strain would be even more severely felt in an extended passage, as when the three weyward Sisters begin the potion that will fetch Macbeth to them. Again, the spoken emphasis is on the capitalised words and the effort of, and/or fixed determination in, speaking can clearly be felt.

> THRICE the BRINDed CAT hath MEW"D
> THRICE and ONCE the HEDGE-Pigge WHIN"D
> HARPier CRIES, 'tis TIME, 'tis TIME.

UNUSUAL ASPECTS OF MAGIC

It's not always easy for the characters to maintain it. And the magic doesn't always come when the character expects it. What is even more interesting is that while the pattern is found a lot in the Comedies, it is usually in much gentler situations, often in songs *(Two Gentlemen of Verona, Merry Wives of Windsor, Much Ado About Nothing, Twelfth Night, The Winters Tale)* and/or simplistic poetry *(Loves Labours Lost* and *As You Like It),* as well as the casket sequence in *The Merchant of Venice.*

It's too easy to dismiss these settings as inferior poetry known as doggerel. But this may be doing the moment and the character a great disservice. The language may be simplistic, but the passion and the magical/ritual intent behind it is wonderfully sincere. It's not just a matter of magic for the sake of magic, as with Pucke and Oberon enchanting mortals and Titania. It's a matter of the human heart's desires too. Orlando, in *As You Like It,* when writing peons of praise to Rosalind suggesting that she is composed of the best parts of the mythical heroines because

> THEREfore HEAVen NATure CHARG"D
> THAT one BODie SHOULD be FILL"D
> WITH all GRACes WIDE enLARG"D

And what could be better than Autolycus *(The Winters Tale)* using magic in his opening song as an extra enticement to trap the unwary into buying all his peddler's goods, ballads, and trinkets.

To help the reader, most magic/ritual lines will be bolded in the Folio text version of the speeches.

ACKNOWLEDGMENTS

Neil dedicated *The Applause First Folio in Modern Type*
"To All Who Have Gone Before"
and there are so many who have gone before in the sharing of Shakespeare through publication. Back to John Heminge and Henry Condell who published *Mr. William Shakespeares Comedies, Histories, & Tragedies* which we now know as The First Folio and so preserved 18 plays of Shakespeare which might otherwise have been lost. As they wrote in their note "To the great Variety of Readers.":

> Reade him, therefore; and againe, and againe : And if then you doe not like him, surely you are in some manifest danger, not to understand him. And so we leave you to other of his Friends, whom if you need, can be your guides: if you neede them not, you can lead yourselves, and others, and such readers we wish him.

I want to thank John Cerullo for believing in these books and helping to spread Neil's vision. I want to thank Rachel Reiss for her invaluable advice and assistance. I want to thank my wife, Maren and my family for giving me support, but above all I want to thank Julie Stockton, Neil's widow, who was able to retrive Neil's files from his old non-internet connected Mac, without which these books would not be possible. Thank you Julie.

Shakespeare for Everyone!

Paul Sugarman, April 2021

Neil Freeman (1941-2015) trained as an actor at the Bristol Old Vic Theatre School. In the world of professional Shakespeare he acted in fourteen of the plays, directed twenty-four, and coached them all many times over.

His groundbreaking work in using the first printings of the Shakespeare texts in performance, on the rehearsal floor and in the classroom led to lectures at the Shakespeare Association of America and workshops at both the ATHE and VASTA, and grants/fellowships from the National Endowment for the Arts (USA), The Social Science and Humanities Research Council (Canada), and York University in Toronto. He prepared and annotated the thirty-six individual Applause First Folio editions of Shakespeare's plays and the complete *The Applause First Folio of Shakespeare in Modern Type.* For Applause he also compiled *Once More Unto the Speech, Dear Friends*, three volumes (Comedy, History and Tragedy) of Shakespeare speeches with commentary and insights to inform audition preparation.

He was Professor Emeritus in the Department of Theatre, Film and Creative Writing at the University of British Columbia, and dramaturg with The Savage God project, both in Vancouver, Canada. He also taught regularly at the National Theatre School of Canada, Concordia University, Brigham Young University.. He had a Founder's Ring (and the position of Master Teacher) with Shakespeare & Company in Lenox, Mass: he was associated with the Will Geer Theatre in Los Angeles; Bard on the Beach in Vancouver; Repercussion Theatre in Montreal; and worked with the Stratford Festival, Canada, and Shakespeare Santa Cruz.

Paul Sugarman is an actor, editor, writer, and teacher of Shakespeare. He is founder of the Instant Shakespeare Company, which has presented annual readings of all of Shakespeare's plays in New York City for over twenty years. For Applause Theatre & Cinema Books, he edited John Russell Brown's publication of *Shakescenes: Shakespeare for Two* and The Applause Shakespeare Library, as well as Neil Freeman's Applause First Folio Editions and *The Applause First Folio of Shakespeare in Modern Type.* He has published pocket editions of all of Shakespeare's plays using the original settings of the First Folio in modern type for Puck Press. Sugarman studied with Kristin Linklater and Tina Packer at Shakespeare & Company where he met Neil Freeman.